...KS OUT IN SHANGHAI

...lap Naval Guns And Chinese Batteries Go Into Action; Scores Of Buildings Aflame

SHANGHAI AGAIN BATTLEGROUND

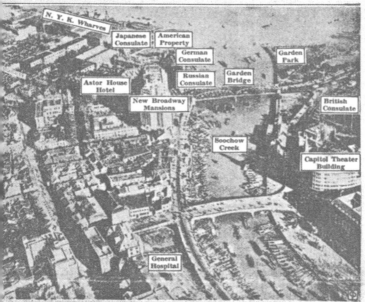

Open warfare is reported to have broken out ...tween Japanese and Chinese on the outskirts of ...hanghai, scene of the 1932 hostilities. Above is a scene of the Chinese city with outstanding landmarks clearly shown.

New Million Dollar Wharf Shelled as Forces Battle in Earnest

1932 HOSTILITIES IN AREA RECALLED

(Associated Press)

SHANGHAI, Aug. 14— (Saturday) — Hostilities between Japanese bluejackets and Chinese army regulars flared today from Shanghai proper all along the ten-mile way to the Woosung forts, where the Whangpoo river flows into the Yangtze.

Casualties, however, though yet indefinite, were believed low. Reports the Japanese were shelling Woosung persisted all night, without confirmation.

Open Warfare
(Associated Press)

SHANGHAI, Aug. 13— Japanese naval guns and Chinese and Japanese land batteries pumped hundreds of shells into their opposing forces in open Shanghai warfare tonight.

An artillery duel along the northern fringe of the city set fire to scores of buildings in the Chinese Kiangswan and Chapei areas. A strong wind threatened a holocaust like that of 1932.

MILLION DOLLAR WHARF BOMBARDED

A Japanese warship bombarded the newly-built $1,500,000 Jukong wharf on the left bank of the Whangpoo river midway

...ATTALION OF BRITISH TROOPS ORDERED TO SHANGHAI AREA REINFORCE GARRISON THERE

Miracles of Life
An Autobiography

Also by J.G. Ballard

The Drowned World
The Voices of Time
The Terminal Beach
The Drought
The Crystal World
The Day of Forever
The Disaster Area
The Atrocity Exhibition
Vermilion Sands
Crash
Concrete Island
High-Rise
Low-Flying Aircraft
The Unlimited Dream Company
The Venus Hunters
Hello America
Myths of the Near Future
Empire of the Sun
The Day of Creation
Running Wild
War Fever
The Kindness of Women
Rushing to Paradise
A User's Guide to the Millennium
Cocaine Nights
Super-Cannes
The Complete Short Stories
Millennium People
Kingdom Come

J.G. Ballard
Miracles of Life
Shanghai to Shepperton
An Autobiography

FOURTH ESTATE • *London*

First published in Great Britain in 2008 by
Fourth Estate
An imprint of HarperCollins*Publishers*
77–85 Fulham Palace Road
London W6 8JB
www.4thestate.co.uk

Visit our authors' blog: www.fifthestate.co.uk

Copyright © J.G. Ballard 2008

1

The right of J.G. Ballard to be identified as the author
of this work has been asserted by him in accordance
with the Copyright, Designs and Patents Act 1988

A catalogue record for this book is
available from the British Library

ISBN 978-0-00-727072-9

All rights reserved. No part of this publication may be
reproduced, transmitted, or stored in a retrieval system,
in any form or by any means, without permission
in writing from Fourth Estate.

Typeset in Minion

Printed in Great Britain by Clays Ltd, St Ives plc

Mixed Sources
Product group from well-managed
forests and other controlled sources
www.fsc.org Cert no. SW-COC-1806
© 1996 Forest Stewardship Council

FSC is a non-profit international organisation established to promote the
responsible management of the world's forests. Products carrying the FSC
label are independently certified to assure consumers that they come
from forests that are managed to meet the social, economic and
ecological needs of present and future generations.

Find out more about HarperCollins and the environment at
www.harpercollins.co.uk/green

To
Fay, Bea and Jim

Contents

PART I

1

Shanghai Arrival (1930)

I was born in Shanghai General Hospital on 15 November 1930, after a difficult delivery that my mother, who was slightly built and slim-hipped, liked to describe to me in later years, as if this revealed something about the larger thoughtlessness of the world. Over dinner she would often tell me that my head was badly deformed during birth, and I feel that for her this partly explained my wayward character as a teenager and young man (doctor friends say that there is nothing remarkable about such a birth). My sister Margaret, born in September 1937, was delivered by Caesarean, but I never heard my mother reflect on its wider significance.

We lived at 31 Amherst Avenue, in the western suburbs of Shanghai, about eight hundred yards beyond the boundary of the International Settlement, but within the larger area controlled by the Shanghai police. The house is still standing and in 1991, when I last visited Shanghai, was the library of the state electronics institute. The International Settlement, with the French Concession of nearly the same size lying along its southern border, extended from the Bund, the line of banks, hotels and trading houses facing the Whangpoo river, for about five miles to the west. Almost all the city's department stores and restaurants, cinemas, radio stations and nightclubs were in the International Settlement, but there were large outlying areas of Shanghai where its industries were located. The five million Chinese inhabitants had free access to the Settlement, and most of the people I saw on its streets were Chinese. I think there were some fifty thousand non-Chinese – British, French, Americans, Germans, Italians, Swiss and Japanese, and a large number of White Russian and Jewish refugees.

Shanghai was not a British colony, as most people imagine, and nothing like Hong Kong and Singapore, which I visited before and after the war and which seemed little more than gunboat anchorages, refuelling bases for the navy rather than vibrant commercial centres, and over-reliant on the pink gin and the loyal toast. Shanghai was one of the largest cities in the world, as it is now, 90 per cent Chinese and 100 per cent Americanised. Bizarre advertising displays – the honour guard of fifty Chinese hunchbacks outside the film premiere of *The Hunchback of Notre Dame* sticks in my mind – were part of the everyday reality of the city, though I sometimes wonder if everyday reality was the one element missing from the city.

With its newspapers in every language and scores of radio stations, Shanghai was a media city before its time, celebrated as the Paris of the Orient and the 'wickedest city in the world', though as a child I knew nothing about the thousands of bars and brothels. Unlimited venture capitalism rode in gaudy style down streets lined with beggars showing off their sores and wounds. Shanghai was important commercially and politically, and for many years was the principal base of the Chinese Communist Party. There were fierce street battles in the 1920s between the Communists and Chiang Kai-shek's Kuomintang forces, followed in the 1930s by frequent terrorist bombings, barely audible, I suspect, against the background music of endless nightclubbing, daredevil air shows and ruthless money-making. Meanwhile, every day, the trucks of the Shanghai Municipal Council roamed the streets collecting the hundreds of bodies of destitute Chinese who had starved to death on Shanghai's pavements, the hardest in the world. Partying, cholera and smallpox somehow coexisted with a small English boy's excited trips in the family Buick to the Country Club swimming pool. Fierce earaches from the infected water were assuaged by unlimited Coca-Cola and ice cream, and the promise that the chauffeur would stop on the way back to Amherst Avenue to buy the latest American comics.

Looking back, and thinking of my own children's upbringing in Shepperton, I realise that I had a lot to take in and digest. Every drive through Shanghai, sitting with the White Russian nanny Vera (supposedly to guard against a kidnap attempt by the chauffeur, though how much of her body this touchy young woman would have laid down for me I can't imagine), I would see something strange and mysterious, but treat it as normal. I think this was the only way in which I could view the bright but bloody kaleidoscope that was Shanghai – the prosperous Chinese businessmen pausing in the Bubbling Well Road to savour a thimble of blood tapped from the neck of a vicious goose tethered to a telephone pole; young Chinese gangsters in American suits beating up a shopkeeper; beggars fighting over their pitches; beautiful White Russian bar-girls smiling at passers-by (I used to wonder what they would be like as my nanny, compared with the morose Vera, who kept a sullen grip on my overactive mind).

Nevertheless, Shanghai struck me as a magical place, a self-generating fantasy that left my own little mind far behind. There was always something odd and incongruous to see: a vast firework display celebrating a new nightclub while armoured cars of the Shanghai police drove into a screaming mob of rioting factory workers; the army of prostitutes in fur coats outside the Park Hotel, 'waiting for friends' as Vera told me. Open sewers fed into the stinking Whangpoo river, and the whole city reeked of dirt, disease and a miasma of cooking fat from the thousands of Chinese food vendors. In the French Concession the huge trams clanked at speed through the crowds, their bells tolling. Anything was possible, and everything could be bought and sold. In many ways, it seems like a stage set, but at the time

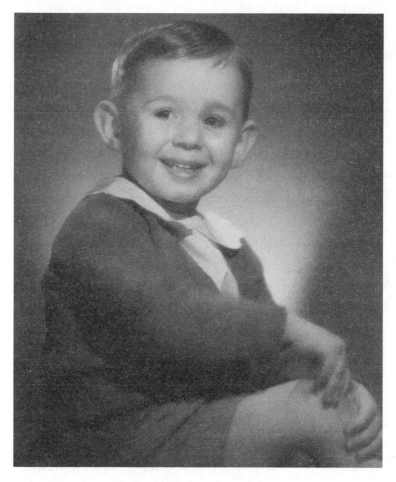

Myself in Shanghai in 1934.

it was real, and I think a large part of my fiction has been an attempt to evoke it by means other than memory.

At the same time there was a strictly formal side to Shanghai life – wedding receptions at the French Club, where I was a page and first tasted cheese canapés, so disgusting that I thought I had caught a terrible new disease. There were race meetings at the Shanghai Racecourse, for which everyone dressed up, and various patriotic gatherings at the British Embassy on the Bund, ultra-formal occasions that involved hours of waiting and nearly drove me mad. My parents held elaborately formal dinner parties, where all the guests were probably drunk and which usually ended for me when some cheerful colleague of my father's found me hiding behind a sofa, feasting on conversations I hadn't a hope of grasping. 'Edna, there's a stowaway on board…'

My mother told me of one reception in the early 1930s when I was introduced to Madame Sun Yat-sen, widow of the man who overthrew the Manchus and became China's first president. But I think my parents probably preferred her sister, Madame Chiang Kai-shek, close friend of America and American big business. My mother was then a pretty young woman in her thirties, and a popular figure at the Country Club. She was once voted the best-dressed woman in Shanghai, but I'm not sure if she took that as a compliment, or whether she really enjoyed her years in Shanghai (roughly 1930 to 1948). Years later, in her sixties, she became a veteran long-haul air traveller, and visited Singapore, Bali and Hong Kong, but not Shanghai. 'It's an industrial city,' she explained, as if that closed the matter.

I suspect that my father, with his passion for H.G. Wells and his belief in modern science as mankind's saviour, enjoyed Shanghai far more. He was always telling the chauffeur to slow down when we passed significant local landmarks – the Radium Institute, where cancer would be cured; the vast Hardoon estate in the centre of the International Settlement, created by an Iraqi property tycoon who was told by a fortune-teller that if he ever stopped building he would die, and who then went on constructing elaborate pavilions all over Shanghai, many of them structures with no doors or interiors. In the confusion of traffic on the Bund he pointed out 'Two-Gun' Cohen, the then famous bodyguard of Chinese warlords, and I gazed with all a small boy's awe at a large American car with armed men standing on the running-boards, Chicago-style. Before the war my father often took me across the Whangpoo river to his company's factory on the eastern bank – I remember still the fearsome noise of the spinning and weaving sheds, the hundreds of massive Lancashire looms each watched by a teenage Chinese girl, ready to stop her machine if a single thread was broken. These peasant girls had long been deafened by the din, but they were their families' only support, and my father opened a school next to the mill where the illiterate girls could learn to read and write and have some hope of becoming office clerks.

This rather impressed me, and I thought long and hard as we sailed back across the river, the China Printing ferry avoiding the dozens of corpses of Chinese whose impoverished relatives were unable to afford a coffin and instead launched them onto the sewage streams from the Nantao outfall. Decked with paper flowers, they drifted to and fro as the busy river traffic of motorised sampans cut through their bobbing regatta.

Shanghai was extravagant but cruel. Even before the Japanese invasion in 1937 there were hundreds of thousands of uprooted Chinese peasants drawn to the city. Few found work, and none found charity. In this era before antibiotics, there were waves of cholera, typhoid and smallpox epidemics, but somehow we survived, partly because the ten servants lived on the premises (in servants' quarters twice the size of my house in Shepperton). The huge consumption of alcohol may have played a prophylactic role; in later years my mother told me that several of my father's English employees drank quietly and steadily through the office day, and then on into the evening. Even so, I caught amoebic dysentery and spent long weeks in Shanghai General Hospital.

On the whole, I was well protected, given the fears of kidnapping. My father was involved in labour disputes with the Communist trade union leaders, and my mother believed that they had threatened to kill him. I assume that he reached some kind of compromise with them, but he kept an automatic pistol between his shirts in a bedroom cupboard, which in due course I found. I often sat on my mother's bed with this small but loaded weapon, practising gunfighter draws and pointing it at my reflection in the full-length mirror. I was lucky enough not to shoot myself, and sensible enough not to boast to my friends at the Cathedral School.

Summers were spent in the northern beach resort of Tsingtao, away from the ferocious heat and stench of Shanghai. Husbands were left behind, and the young wives had a great time with the Royal Navy officers on shore leave from their ships. There is a photograph of a dozen dressed-up wives each sitting in a wicker chair with a suntanned, handsomely smiling officer behind her. Who were the hunters, and who the trophies?

Amherst Avenue was a road of large Western-style houses that ran for a mile or so beyond the perimeter of the International Settlement. From the roof of our house we looked across the open countryside, an endless terrain of paddy fields, small villages, canals and cultivated land that ran in the direction of what later became Lunghua internment camp, some five miles to the south. The house was a three-storey, half-timbered structure in the Surrey stockbroker style. Each foreign nationality in Shanghai built its houses in its own idiom – the French built Provençal villas and art deco mansions, the Germans Bauhaus white boxes, the English their half-timbered fantasies of golf-club elegance, exercises in a partly bogus nostalgia that I recognised decades later when I visited Beverly Hills. But all the houses, like 31 Amherst Avenue, tended to have American interiors –

overly spacious kitchens, room-sized pantries with giant refrigerators, central heating and double glazing, and a bathroom for every bedroom. This meant a complete physical privacy. I never saw my parents naked or in bed together, and always used the bath and lavatory next to my own bedroom. By contrast, my own children shared almost every intimacy with my wife and me, the same taps, soap and towels, and I hope the same frankness about the body and its all too human functions.

But physical privacy may have been more difficult for my parents to achieve in our Shanghai home than I could have imagined as a boy. There were ten Chinese servants – No. 1 Boy (in his thirties and the only fluent English speaker), his assistant No. 2 Boy, No. 1 Coolie, for the heavy housework, his assistant No. 2 Coolie, a cook, two amahs (hard-fisted women with tiny bound feet, who never smiled or showed the least signs of affability), a gardener, a chauffeur and a nightwatchman who patrolled the drive and garden while we slept. Lastly there was a European nanny, generally a White Russian young woman who lived in the main house with us.

The cook's son was a boy of my age, whose name my mother remembered until her nineties. I tried desperately to make friends with him, but never succeeded. He was not allowed into the main garden, and refused to follow me when I invited him to climb the trees with me. He spent his time in the alley between the main house and the servants' quarters and his only toy was an empty Klim tin that had once held powdered milk. There were three holes in its lid, through which he would drop small stones, then remove the lid and peer inside. He would do this for hours, mystifying me completely and challenging my infinitely short attention span. Aware that I had a bedroom filled with expensive British and German toys (ordered every September from Hamleys in London), I made a selection of cars, aeroplanes, lead soldiers and model battleships and carried them down to him. He seemed bemused by these strange objects, so I left him to explore them. Two hours later I crept back and found him surrounded by the untouched toys, dropping stones into his tin. I realise now that this was probably a gambling game. The toys had been a genuine gift, but when I went to bed that night I found that they had all been returned. I hope that this shy and likeable Chinese boy survived the war, and often think of him with his tin and little pebbles, far away in a universe of his own.

This large number of servants, entirely typical among the better-off Western families, was made possible by the extremely low wages paid. No. 1 Boy received about £30 a year (perhaps £1000 at today's values) and the coolies and amahs about £10 a year. They lived rent-free but had to buy their own food. Periodically a delegation led by No. 1 Boy would approach my mother and father as they sipped their whisky sodas on the veranda and explain that the price of rice had risen again, and presumably my father increased their pay accordingly. Even after the Japanese seizure of the

International Settlement in December 1941 my father employed the full complement of servants, though business activity had fallen sharply. After the war he explained to me that the servants had nowhere to go and would probably have perished if he had dismissed them.

Curiously, this human concern ran hand in hand with social conventions that seem unthinkable today. We addressed the servants as 'No. 1 Boy' or 'No. 2 Coolie' and never by their real names. My mother might say, 'Boy, tell No. 2 Coolie to sweep the drive…' or 'No. 2 Boy, switch on the hall lights…' I did the same from a very early age. No. 1 Boy, answering my father, would say 'Master, I tell No. 2 Boy buy fillet steak from compradore' – the lavishly stocked food emporium in the Avenue Joffre which supplied our kitchen.

Given the harsh facts of existence on the streets of Shanghai, and the famine, floods and endless civil war that had ravaged their villages, the servants may have been reasonably content, aware that thousands of destitute Chinese roamed the streets of Shanghai, ready to do anything to find work. Every morning when I was driven to school I would notice fresh coffins left by the roadside, sometimes miniature coffins decked with paper flowers containing children of my own age. Bodies lay in the streets of downtown Shanghai, wept over by Chinese peasant women, ignored in the rush of passers-by. Once, when my father took me to his office in the Szechuan Road, near the

Bund, a Chinese family had spent the night huddling against the steel grille at the top of the entrance steps. They had been driven away by the security guards, leaving a dead baby against the grille, its life ended by disease or the fierce cold. In the Bubbling Well Road our car had to halt when the rickshaw coolie in front of us suddenly stopped, lowered his cotton trousers and leant forward over his shafts, defecating a torrent of yellow liquid at the roadside, to be stepped in by the passing crowds and carried all over Shanghai, bearing dysentery or cholera into every factory, shop and office.

As a small boy aged 5 or 6 I must have accepted all this without a thought, along with the backbreaking labour of the coolies unloading the ships along the Bund, middle-aged men with bursting calf veins, swaying and sighing under enormous loads slung from their shoulder-yokes, moving a slow step at a time towards the nearby godowns, the large warehouses of the Chinese merchants. Afterwards they would squat with a bowl of rice and a cabbage leaf that somehow gave them the energy to bear these monstrous loads. In the Nanking Road the Chinese begging boys ran after our car and tapped the windows, crying 'No mama, no papa, no whisky soda...' Had they picked up the cry thrown back at them ironically by Europeans who didn't care?

When I was 6, before the Japanese invasion in 1937, an old beggar sat down with his back to the wall at the foot of our drive, at the point where our car paused before turning into Amherst Avenue. I looked at him from the rear seat of our

15

Buick, a thin, ancient man dressed in rags, undernourished all his life and now taking his last breaths. He rattled a Craven A tin at passers-by, but no one gave him anything. After a few days he was visibly weaker, and I asked my mother if No. 2 Coolie would take the old man a little food. Tired of my pestering, she eventually gave in, and said that Coolie would take the old man a bowl of soup. The next day it snowed, and the old man was covered with a white quilt. I remember telling myself that he would feel warmer under this soft eiderdown. He stayed there, under his quilt, for several days, and then he was gone.

Forty years later I asked my mother why we had not fed this old man at the bottom of our drive, and she replied: 'If we had fed him, within two hours there would have been fifty beggars there.' In her way, she was right. Enterprising Europeans had brought immense prosperity to Shanghai, but even Shanghai's wealth could never feed the millions of destitute Chinese driven towards the city by war and famine. I still think of that old man, of a human being reduced to such a desperate end a few yards from where I slept in a warm bedroom surrounded by my expensive German toys. But as a boy I was easily satisfied by a small act of kindness, a notional bowl of soup that I probably knew at the time was no more than a phrase on my mother's lips. By the time I was 14 I had become as fatalistic about death, poverty and hunger as the Chinese. I knew that kindness alone would feed few mouths and save no lives.

Myself aged 5 at my riding school in Shanghai.

I remember very little before the age of 5 or 6, when I joined the junior form of the Cathedral School for boys. The school was run on English lines with a syllabus aimed at the School Certificate examinations or their pre-war equivalent, heavily dominated by Latin and scripture classes. The masters were English, and we were made to work surprisingly hard, given the nightclub and dinner-party ethos that ruled the parents' lives. There were two hours of Latin every other day and a great deal of homework. The headmaster was a Church of England clergyman called the Reverend Matthews, a sadist who was free not only with his cane but with his fists, brutally slapping quite small boys. I'm certain that today he would be prosecuted for child abuse and assault. Miraculously I escaped his wrath, though I soon guessed why. My father was the chairman of a prominent English company, and later vice-chairman of the British Residents Association. I noticed that the Reverend Matthews only caned and slapped the boys from more modest backgrounds. One or two were beaten and humiliated almost daily, and I'm still surprised that the parents never complained. Bizarrely, this was all part of the British stiff-upper-lip tradition, no match as it would turn out for another violent tradition, bushido, and the ferocious violence meted out by Japanese NCOs to the soldiers under their command.

When the Reverend Matthews was interned he underwent a remarkable sea change: he abandoned his clerical collar and spent hours sunbathing in a deckchair, and even became something of a ladies' man, as if at last able to throw off the disguise imposed on him by a certain kind of English self-delusion.

Outside school I remember a great many children's parties, every child escorted by its refugee nanny, a chance for White Russian and German Jewish girls to exchange gossip. During school holidays we would drive every morning to the Country Club, where I spent hours in the swimming pool with my friends. I was a strong swimmer, and won a small silver spoon for coming first in a diving competition, though

I wonder if the prize was awarded to me or to my parents.

At home I spent a great deal of time on my own. Social life in pre-war Shanghai was a career occupation for my mother, playing tennis at the Country Club, bridge with her friends, shopping and lunching in the downtown hotels. In the evenings there were dinner parties and nightclub visits. Often my mother would help me with my Latin homework, but much of the day I was alone in a large house where the Chinese servants never looked at me and never spoke to me, while the nanny read my mother's novels and played dance music on the radiogram. I would sometimes listen to one of the dozens of English-language radio stations (I liked to phone in record requests under the alias 'Ace') or play chess with the nanny; my father taught me to win, and I taught the nannies to lose. The succession of White Russian girls must have been bored to death by me, and one of them told me that the sound of thunder that startled me was 'the voice of God – he's angry with you, James.' I remember being unsettled by this for years. For some reason I almost believed her.

Now and then I would go with my mother or the nanny to the cinema, one of the vast art deco theatres that loomed over Shanghai. The first film I saw was *Snow White*, which frightened the wits out of me. The wicked queen, the purest essence of evil radiating across the auditorium, reminded me too much of my friends' mothers when they tired of me rearranging their furniture.

Most of the children's books I read, such as the *Arabian*

Nights, the Grimms' fairy tales and *The Water-Babies*, were deeply disturbing, with illustrations inspired by the Pre-Raphaelites and Beardsley, full of airless gothic interiors and lantern-lit forests. They probably prepared me for the surrealists. I read children's versions of *Gulliver's Travels* and *Robinson Crusoe*, which I loved, especially *Crusoe*, and I can still hear the sound of waves on his beach. I devoured American comics, which were on sale everywhere in Shanghai and read by all the English boys – *Buck Rogers*, *Flash Gordon* and, later, *Superman*. *Terry and the Pirates* was my favourite, about an American mercenary pilot in the Far East, part of it set in the Shanghai where I lived. Later I read American bestsellers, such as *All This and Heaven Too*, *Babbitt*, *Anthony Adverse* and *Gone With the Wind*. My parents subscribed to a number of magazines – *Life*, *Time*, the *New Yorker*, *Saturday Evening Post* and so on, and I spent hours turning their pages and revelling in their American optimism.

Then there were the *Chums* and *Boy's Own Paper* annuals, aggressive compendiums of patriotic derring-do. A.A. Milne and the *Just William* series together portrayed a mythical middle-class England, a Home Counties, *Peter Pan* world far more remote from reality than *Life* and *Time* were from the realities of American life. However, it seemed to be confirmed by the British doctors, architects, managers and clergymen I met in Shanghai. They might have driven American cars and had American refrigerators, but in speech and manner they weren't too far from the doctors and schoolmasters I came across in my reading.

All this gave the British adults in Shanghai a certain authority, which they lost completely a few years later after the sinking of the battleships *Repulse* and *Prince of Wales* and the surrender of Singapore. The British lost a respect which they never recovered, as I discovered when Chinese shop-keepers, French dentists and Sikh school-bus drivers made disparaging remarks about British power. The dream of empire died when Singapore surrendered without a fight and our aircraft proved no match for the highly trained Zero pilots. Even at the age of 11 or 12 I knew that no amount of patriotic newsreels would put the Union Jack jigsaw together again. From then on I was slightly suspicious of all British adults.

My closest friends were an English family called the Kendall-Wards, who lived at the far end of Amherst Avenue, and were a happy exception to every rule of expatriate English life. During the holidays I would cycle over and spend most of the day with them. There were three brothers, whom I remember well, but it was the parents who made a powerful and lasting impact on me. Mr Kendall-Ward was a senior executive with the Shanghai Power Company, but he and his wife were free spirits who rarely mixed on a social level with other British residents. The father was a model railway enthusiast, and the enclosed veranda on the first floor, a room some thirty feet long, was filled with a vast landscape of tunnels, hills, villages, lakes and railway lines, laid out on a waist-high platform fitted with trapdoors through which he would emerge without warning to make some track adjustment. Once he had filled this huge space he began to colonise the nearby rooms off the veranda, building narrow ledges around the walls which carried the miniature railway lines ever deeper into the house.

Mrs Kendall-Ward presided over this friendly chaos, welcoming and cheerful, surrounded by four Airedale dogs, nursing a new baby and asking me about the latest news from downtown Shanghai. She listened with apparent interest as I told her in detail about a new French or Italian warship moored off the Bund. She spoke fluent Chinese to the amahs, an unheard-of skill that amazed me, and addressed them by their names. Uniquely among Shanghai residents, she employed only women servants, some six or seven amahs. According to my mother, this was an act of charity on the Kendall-Wards' part – these middle-aged spinsters would otherwise have found it difficult to survive.

The Kendall-Ward home was the complete opposite of 31 Amherst Avenue, and an influence that has lasted all my life. My mother was amiable but distant with any friends I brought home. Relations between parents and children were far more formal in the 1930s and 1940s, and our house reflected this, an almost cathedral-like space of polished parquet floors and blackwood furniture. By contrast the Kendall-Ward home was an untidy nest, full of barking dogs, arguing amahs and the sound of Mr Kendall-Ward's power saws slicing though plywood, the three brothers and myself roller-skating through the rooms and generally running wild. I knew that this was the right way to bring up children. Appearances counted for nothing, and everyone was encouraged to follow their own notions, however hare-brained. Mrs Kendall-Ward openly breastfed her baby, something only Chinese women did. If she was driving us around Shanghai in the family Packard, and stopped to buy American comics for her sons, she always included a comic for me, something I noticed that neither my own mother nor any of the other English mothers ever did. Her kindness and good nature I remember vividly seventy years later. I was rarely unhappy at home, but I was always happy at the Kendall-Wards, and I think that I was aware of the difference at the time.

2

Japanese Invasion (1937)

In 1937 the street spectacle that so enthralled a small English boy was bathed in a far more chilling light. Led by its military chiefs, and with the silent blessing of the Emperor, Japan launched a full-scale invasion of China. Its armies seized all the coastal cities, including Shanghai, though they did not enter the International Settlement. For several months there was bitter fighting in the outlying areas of the city, especially the Chapei and Nantao suburbs. Relentless Japanese bombing and naval bombardment from their warships in the Whangpoo river levelled large areas of Shanghai. For the first time in the history of warfare a coordinated air, sea and land assault was launched against Chiang Kai-shek's Chinese armies, who greatly outnumbered the Japanese, but were poorly led by corrupt cronies of Chiang and his wife.

One bomb, dropped by accident from a Chinese aircraft, struck the Great World Amusement Park near the racecourse in the heart of the International Settlement, which was filled with refugees from the outlying districts. The bomb killed a thousand people, at the time the largest number of casualties ever caused by a single bomb. The Chinese pushed the Japanese back towards the river, until they were fighting from trenches that filled with water at high tide. But the Japanese prevailed, and Chiang's armies withdrew into the vast interior of China. The new national capital became Chungking, 900 miles to the west.

There was desperate fighting in the open countryside only a mile from our home. At one point artillery shells from the rival Chinese and Japanese batteries were passing over our roof, and my parents closed the house and moved with the servants to the comparative safety of a rented house in the French Concession.

Curiously, the house we moved to had a drained swimming pool in its garden. It must have been the first drained pool I had seen, and it struck me as strangely significant in a way I have never fully grasped. My parents decided not to fill the pool, and it lay in the garden like a mysterious empty presence. I would walk through the unmown grass and stare down at its canted floor. I could hear the bombing and gunfire all around Shanghai, and see the vast pall of smoke that lay over the city, but the drained pool remained apart. In the coming years I would see a great many drained and half-drained pools, as British residents left Shanghai for Australia and Canada, or the assumed 'safety' of Hong Kong and Singapore, and they all seemed as mysterious as that first pool in the French Concession. I was unaware of the obvious symbolism that British power was ebbing away, because no one thought so at the time, and faith in the British Empire was at its jingoistic height. Right up to, and beyond, Pearl Harbor it was taken for granted that the dispatch of a few Royal Navy warships would send the Japanese scuttling back to Tokyo Bay. I think now that the drained pool represented the unknown, a concept that had played no part in my life. Shanghai in the 1930s was full of extravagant fantasies, but these spectacles were designed to promote a new hotel or airport, a new department store, nightclub or dog-racing track. Nothing was unknown.

Once the Chinese armies had withdrawn, life in Shanghai resumed as if little had changed. The Japanese surrounded the city, but made no attempt to confront the contingents of British, French and American soldiers, or to interfere with their warships in the river facing the Bund. The Japanese cruiser *Idzumo*, a veteran of the Great War, sat in midstream, but Shanghai's hotels, bars and nightclubs were as busy as ever.

With their villages and rice fields destroyed, thousands of destitute peasants from the Yangtze basin flocked to Shanghai and fought to enter the International Settlement. They were viciously repelled by the Japanese soldiers and by the British-run police force. I saw many Chinese who had been bayoneted and lay on the ground among their blood-stained rice sacks. Violence was so pervasive that my parents and the various nannies never tried to shield me from all the brutality going on. I knew that the Japanese were capable of losing their tempers and lunging with their fixed bayonets into the crowds pressing around them. Later, when I was eight or nine and began my long cycle rides around Shanghai, I was careful to avoid provoking the Japanese soldiers. They always waved me through the checkpoints, as they did the Europeans and Americans. Sometimes they would check our family Buick, but only when the chauffeur was driving.

I assume that the Japanese leadership had decided that Shanghai was of more value to them as a thriving commercial and industrial centre, and were not yet prepared to risk a confrontation with the Western powers. Most of my earliest memories date from this period, and life in Shanghai seemed to be an endless round of parties, lavish weddings, swimming club galas, film shows laid on by the British Embassy, military tattoos staged on the racecourse, glossy film premieres, all under the bayonets of the Japanese soldiers who guarded the perimeter checkpoints around the Settlement.

As soon as the fighting ended, the Cathedral Boys' School moved from the cloisters of Shanghai Cathedral, not far from the Great World Amusement Park, and took over part of the Cathedral Girls' School on the western edge of the International Settlement. I could now cycle to school, and no longer needed to be chauffeured in the family car, with the nanny keeping an interfering watch over me. I began to take longer and longer rides around the city, using the excuse that I was visiting the Kendall-Wards or other friends. I liked to cycle down the Nanking Road, lined with Shanghai's biggest department stores, Sincere's and the vast Sun and Sun Sun emporiums, dodging in and out of the huge trams with their clanging bells that forced their way through the rickshaws and pedestrians.

Everywhere I turned, a cruel and lurid world surged around me. Shanghai lived above all on the street, the beggars showing their wounds, the gangsters and pickpockets, the dying rattling their Craven A tins, the Chinese dragon ladies in ankle-length mink coats who terrified me with their stares, the hawkers wok-frying delicious treats which I could never buy because I never carried any money, starving peasant families and thousands of con men and crooks. Weird quarter-tone music wailed from Chinese theatres and bars, fireworks crackled around a wedding party, a radio blared out the speeches of Generalissimo Chiang, interrupted by commercials for a Japanese beer. I took all this in at a glance, the polluted and exciting air I breathed. If they were in the mood, the British soldiers in their sandbag emplacements would invite me into their dark interior world, where they lounged about cleaning their equipment. I liked these Tommies with their strange accents I had never heard before, and they let me clean their rifles and use the pull-throughs to ream the rust from their barrels, then gave me a bronze cap badge as a present. They told wonderfully broad stories of their service in India and Africa, and Shanghai to them was just another name on the map. I explored almost every corner of the International Settlement, and schoolfriends and I would play games of hide-and-seek that covered the whole city and could last for months. It amazes me now that none of us ever came to any harm, and I assume that the thousands of plain-clothes Chinese police agents in effect kept watch over us, warning away any petty crook tempted to steal our cycles or pull the shoes from our feet.

In fact, the greatest danger we faced probably came from the Sunday afternoon trips we took with our parents and their friends to the recent battlegrounds to the south and west of Shanghai. Convoys of chauffeur-driven Buicks and Chryslers would move through the stricken land, wives in their silky best. The battlefields must have reminded some of the older British of the Somme, with their endless networks of eroded trenches, crumbling earth blockhouses and abandoned villages. Around our feet when we stepped from the cars was the bright gold of spent cartridges, lengths of machine-gun ammunition, webbing and backpacks. Dead horses lay by the roadside, enormous ribcages open to the sky, and in the canals were dead Chinese soldiers, legs stirring as the current flowed through the reeds. There was a feast of military souvenirs, but I was never allowed to keep even a bayonet – many European sightseers had been killed, and a boy at school lost a hand when a grenade exploded. Then the convoy would roll on, carrying everyone back to the safety of the International Settlement and large gins at the Country Club.

Another treasure hunt to which I very keenly looked forward took place when we visited friends of my parents in the countryside to the west of Shanghai. They held large lunch parties, after which the children were left to themselves while the nannies gossiped and the chauffeurs polished their cars. I would slip away, duck through a gap in the fence and run across two dried-out rice paddies to an abandoned Chinese military airfield. There was a single empty hangar, but on the edge of the airfield, forgotten in the long grass, was the shell of a Chinese fighter plane. I managed to climb into the cockpit, and would sit on the low metal seat, surrounded by the grimy controls. It was a magical experience, more exciting than any funfair ride, not because I could imagine the sounds of battle, machine-gun fire and rushing air, but because I was alone with this stricken but mysterious craft, an intact dream of flight. I visited it three or four times, whenever there was a lunch party, and if one of the adults saw me slipping through the fence I would say that I was looking for a lost kite, which in a sense I was. On my last visit, as I stepped out onto the airfield, several Japanese soldiers were inspecting the hangar and ordered me away. Years later, this small airfield became the site of Shanghai International Airport. In 1991, when I stepped down the gangway of the Airbus that had brought me to Shanghai from Hong Kong, I could almost sense the presence of a small boy still sitting in his Chinese fighter, unaware of the years that had flown past him.

My sister Margaret (now Margaret Richardson, until recently director of the Soane Museum) was born in 1937, but the seven-year gap between us meant that she never became a childhood friend. When I was 10 she was still a toddler. I was busy with my exploration of the International Settlement, and my prolonged but unsuccessful attempts to fraternise with the Japanese soldiers who manned the checkpoints into the city. There was a strain of melancholy in the Japanese that I responded to, although I myself was never sad. I had a natural optimism that I only lost when I arrived in England, and I was probably hyperactive, in today's jargon. I was always on the go, whether playing my intense private games with my model soldiers, leading the Kendall-Ward boys on an expedition to a ruined factory I had discovered, or exploring some unknown corner of the Shanghai suburbs.

The most visible features of the flat landscape beyond Amherst Avenue were the family burial mounds built onto the retaining walls of the paddy fields. The water table was only three feet below the surface of the ground, and none of the villagers buried their dead beneath the soil (at one time I went through a well-digging phase, sinking half a dozen wells into the flowerbeds in our garden until the gardener protested). The mounds could be six to ten feet high, a pyramid of coffins covered with soil that the heavy rains would wash away. Unless regularly maintained, the coffins would emerge into the daylight.

There was a burial mound on the edge of an abandoned paddy field three hundred yards from our house. One day, on my way back from school, I made a small detour to the mound, climbed up the rotting pyramid and peered into one of the lidless coffins. The skeleton of a forgotten rice farmer lay on what seemed like a mattress of silk – the soil around him had been endlessly washed and rinsed by the rains. Years later, as a Cambridge medical student, I would sleep in my college room with my anatomy skeleton in a coffin-like pine box under my bed. I was told that the skeleton's modest height did not mean it was that of a child – most anatomy skeletons were those of south-east Asian peasants.

Despite my heroic cycle trips, my insulation from Chinese life was almost complete. I lived in Shanghai for fifteen years and never learned a word of Chinese. Although my father had a large Chinese workforce, and at one point took Chinese lessons, he never uttered a syllable of Chinese to any of our servants. I never had a Chinese meal, either at home or during the many hotel and restaurant visits with my parents and their friends. We ate roast beef and roast lamb, American waffles and syrup, ice cream sundaes. My first Chinese meal was in England after the war. Today, British and European émigrés to the third world have been educated by television to take an interest in the local history and culture – its cuisine, architecture, folklore and customs. This was not the case in 1930s Shanghai, in part because there was so little of that history and culture available in Shanghai, and partly because of the standoffishness of the Chinese.

And perhaps, after all, too little was hidden in Shanghai. Even as a 10-year-old who had known nothing else, the extreme poverty of the Chinese, the deaths and disease and orphans left to starve in doorways, unsettled me as it must have unsettled my parents. I assume that both had emotionally distanced themselves from what they saw in the Shanghai streets. There were many foreign-run charities which they actively supported, but they probably knew there was very little that even the most sympathetic Westerners could do for the millions of destitute Chinese. My mother travelled everywhere in her chauffeur-driven car, and may well have seen less of poverty than her forever-cycling son. There were also huge numbers of destitute European refugees – White Russians, German and eastern European Jews fleeing from the Nazi threat, English expats down on their luck, political refugees from all over the world who needed no visas to enter Shanghai. As the thousands of bars and nightclubs toasted the even better years to come, and the dancers continued to dance, I cycled up and down the Avenue Foch and the Bubbling Well Road, always on the lookout for something new and rarely disappointed.

In Shanghai the fantastic, which for most people lies

inside their heads, lay all around me, and I think now that my main effort as a boy was to find the real in all this make-believe. In some ways I went on doing this when I came to England after the war, a world that was almost too real. As a writer I've treated England as if it were a strange fiction, and my task has been to elicit the truth, just as my childhood self did when faced with honour guards of hunchbacks and temples without doors.

Meanwhile, there was a host of treats to look forward to: children's parties with their conjurors and tumblers; the gymkhana at the riding school where I would pretend to steer my docile nag around a figure-of-eight course, all the beast could remember; the premiere of *The Wizard of Oz*, attended by the whole school; Saturday ice cream sundaes at the Chocolate Shop, a happy bedlam of small boys, amahs and exhausted nannies; the American Hell-Drivers at the racecourse, crashing their cars through burning walls; a visit to the Chinese theatre in the Old City, a nightmare of ear-splitting gongs and grimacing masks; a trip to the jai alai stadium with its ferocious Chinese gamblers and Filipino players with huge scoop-rackets that seemed to propel the ball at rifle speed (the fastest ball game in the world, my father said, which greatly impressed me, as did anything that was fastest, tallest, highest and deepest); chasing the trucks that carried the ever-friendly US Marines, cheering me on until my front wheel jammed in a tramline and I pitched headlong among the Chinese shoppers outside Sincere's; and regular trips to see the *Idzumo* moored off the Bund. Yet with all these excitements, I still found myself thinking for a few moments at least of the Chinese beggar-children on the ash-tips near the chemical works by the Avenue Joffre, picking away in the coldest weather for the smallest lumps of coke. It was the gap between their lives and mine that bothered me, but there seemed no way of bridging it.

That gap, and Shanghai itself, would close sooner than I could have guessed.

3

War in Europe (1939)

In September 1939 the European war began, and quickly reached across the world to Shanghai. Outwardly, our lives continued as before, but soon there were empty places in my class at school, as families sold up and left for Hong Kong and Singapore. My father spent a great deal of time listening to the short-wave radio broadcasts from England, which brought news of the sinking of HMS *Hood* and the hunt for the *Bismarck*, then later of Dunkirk and the Battle of Britain. School was often interrupted so that we could visit one of the cinemas for screenings of British newsreels, thrilling spectacles that showed battleships in line ahead, and Spitfires downing Heinkels over London. Fund-raising drives were held at the Country Club, and I remember the proud announcement that the British residents in Shanghai had financed their first Spitfire. There was constant patriotic activity on all sides. The German and Italian communities mounted their own propaganda campaigns, and the swastika flew from the flagpoles of the German school and the

German radio station, which put out a steady stream of pro-Nazi programmes.

Newsreels soon became the dominant weapon in this information war, many of them screened at night against the sides of buildings, watched by huge crowds of passing pedestrians. I think I saw the European war as a newsreel war, only taking place on the silver square above my head, its visual conventions decided by the resources and limits of the war cameraman, as I would now put it, though even my 10-year-old eyes could sense the difference between an authentic newsreel and one filmed on manoeuvres. The real, whether war or peace, was something you saw filmed in newsreels, and I wanted the whole of Shanghai to be filmed.

The English adults began to talk now about 'home', a rose-pink view of England that seemed to consist of the West End of London, Shaftesbury Avenue and the Troc, a glittery sparkle of first nights and dancing till dawn, overlaid by a comfortable Beverley Nichols world of market towns and thatched roofs. Did my parents and their friends convince themselves, or were they keeping their morale up? They played cricket at the Country Club, usually after too many gins, and subscribed to *Punch*, but they drove American cars and cooled their vermouth in American refrigerators. They talked about retiring, not to the Cotswolds, but to South Africa, with its abundant cheap servants. I think that, despite themselves, they had been internationalised by Shanghai, and their Noël Coward/*Cavalcade* notions of England were a nostalgic folk memory (when we arrived in England in 1946, some of us were assumed to be American, and not because of our accents).

This probably explains why many of the British residents stayed on in Shanghai even though it was clear that war against Japan was imminent. There was also the firm belief, racist to a large extent, that while the Japanese had easily routed the Chinese armies they would be no match for the Royal Navy and the Royal Air Force. Japanese pilots flew inferior planes and had notoriously bad eyesight, according to cocktail-party wisdom. But the blinkered vision lay in the eyes of the British, a strange self-delusion bearing in mind that my parents and their friends had seen the ruthless courage of the Japanese soldiers and the skill of their pilots at first hand since 1937.

In many ways life in Shanghai instilled a kind of unconscious optimism in the European residents. Living in a centre of unlimited entrepreneurial capitalism, everyone believed that anything was possible. In the last resort, money would buy off any danger. The vast metropolis where I was born had been raised within not much more than thirty years from a collection of low-lying swamps (selected by the Manchu rulers as a sign of their contempt), and attracted bemused visitors from all over the world, from George Bernard Shaw to Auden and Isherwood.

There was also a pleasantly tolerant climate of what now seems unbelievably heavy drinking. When I mentioned the 'two-martini lunch' to my mother at the time I was writing *Empire of the Sun*, she retorted: 'Five martinis…' As a small boy I took it for granted that drinks were served at any hour, and the pantry cupboards resembled a medium-sized off-licence, with shelves of gin and whisky bottles. Many of the people my parents knew remained slightly drunk all day, and I remember the family dentist whose breath always reeked of something stronger than mouth-rinse. But this was common in the Far East, partly a social convention, an extension of wine with one's meals to every other human activity, and partly a response to living in a city without a museum or gallery, and where the houses in the nearby streets were thirty years younger than the residents. I asked my mother about drugs, and she insisted that no one in her circle took them, though she knew people who were morphine addicts. But bridge, alcohol and adultery are the royal cement that holds societies together, and too many sedative drugs would have shut down a large part of Shanghai. In England in the 1960s my parents were abstemious drinkers, having a whisky soda before dinner and a single glass of wine, at a time when I was drinking half a bottle of Scotch a day. My mother was rarely ill and lived to the age of 93.

My earliest childhood writings began in the late 1930s, perhaps as a response to the greater tension I sensed among the adults around me. The outbreak of war in Europe and,

later, the fall of France left my parents distracted and less
interested in what I was doing. My sister, aged three, irritated
me immensely, and I tried to devise entire days when I never
set eyes on her. Breakfast was always a problem, with school
deciding when I sat down to my mango and scrambled egg,
and having to endure my sister's babbling across the table.
With a small boy's logic, I took advantage of Mr Kendall-
Ward's carpentry room to construct a large plywood screen
which I placed in the centre of the dining table. I equipped it
with a spyhole through which I could ferociously keep watch
on my astonished sister, and a miniature hatch cover that
I would flick into place when she noticed my staring eye.
Amazingly, my parents took all this with good humour, but
they drew the line when I joined them for lunch with friends
and arrived dragging my huge screen, which I urged No. 2
Boy to set up on the table.

But clearly I needed to be alone. I was always a keen storyteller, and enjoyed school essays when there was a free choice
and I could describe some important event, real or imaginary. At the Cathedral School the standard penalty for small
infringements was 'lines', which involved copying out a set
number of pages from a worthy book we were studying. So
it would be 'Maxted, five pages; Ballard, eight pages,' a con-
siderable chore on top of one's regular homework. The
choice of text would usually be one of the Victorian writers
in the school library – G.A. Henty, Dickens (we read *A Tale
of Two Cities*, which I loathed for its deep gloom), or Charles

Kingsley. One evening at home, laboriously transcribing endless paragraphs from Kingsley's *Westward Ho!*, a tale about the Spanish Main, it occurred to me that I could get along much more quickly if I invented the story and text myself. So I wrote a swashbuckling pirate yarn. Like all the boys, I took it for granted that the masters never read our lines, but the day after handing in my penalty pages the Reverend Matthews pointed sternly to me in front of the scripture class and said: 'Next time, Ballard, don't copy your lines from some trashy novel...' This was my first review, and recognition of a kind, and was a spur to more efforts for my own amusement. It may have set my fiction in its subversive mode.

Bridge parties seemed to take place continuously at 31 Amherst Avenue, involving two foursomes of my mother's women friends. I would sit on the stairs, listening carefully to the flow of bids – 'One diamond, two hearts, three no trumps, double...' – utterly baffled by the apparent lack of any logic in the sequences. Eventually, at the age of 10 or so, I nagged my mother into explaining the rules of contract bridge to me, including a few of the conventions, which were a code within a code. So thrilled was I at grasping the mystery of bridge that I decided to write a 'book' explaining the game to anyone as baffled as I had been. I filled about half an exercise book, furnishing it with diagrams in the approved style, and I remember clearly that there was even a section on 'psychic bidding', nothing to do with ESP but a form of bluff.

I haven't played bridge for fifty years, but that little explanatory text might well have given me a taste as a writer for the decoding of mystery.

The summer holidays in Tsingtao came to an end, but I still have strong memories of a pretty, almost Riviera-style beach resort. Tsingtao had been a German naval base at the start of the Great War, and in a small cove near our hotel were the rotting hulls of two German submarines, lying with their bows on the sand like rusting dinosaurs. The Germans had built a huge network of forts into the cliffs, and these were a popular tourist attraction. My mother and I joined one tour group, and we were guided through the dark, cathedral-like vaults. Immense lifts raised the heavy guns to the firing platforms, and through the gloom of damp concrete I could see upper galleries that gave way to further galleries and observation posts, and later reminded me of Piranesi's *Prisons*. The Royal Navy bombarded the forts before its capture of Tsingtao, and the Chinese guides were very proud of the bloody handprints which they claimed were those of German gunners driven mad by the British bombardment.

My memories of Tsingtao are extremely pleasant, but my mother often told me that when I was a baby (in the summer of 1931 or 1932) the amah pushing my pram missed her footing on the grassy slope above the cliffs and lost control of the pram. It sped downhill towards the cliff's edge, where a chance British visitor ran forward and caught the pram before it went over the edge. Presumably he reported back to my mother at her hotel, though she never explained to me why a middle-aged Chinese woman, hobbling on her bound feet, should have been given charge of a large pram and told to walk along a cliff edge. Hitchcock would have revelled in the scene, but I think there is a simpler explanation. Parents in the 1930s took what now seems a remarkably detached view of their children, whose welfare if they could afford it was assigned to servants, whatever the hazards. My parents had been born in the first decade of the 20th century, long before antibiotics and public health concerns for vitamin-enriched foods, clean air and water. Childhood, for families of any income, was a gamble with disease and early death. All this devalued the entire experience of childhood, and emphasised the importance of being adult, an achievement in its own right. Children were an appendage to the parents, somewhere between the servants and an obedient labrador, and were never seen as a significant measure of a family's health or the centre of its life. My mother claimed not to have known of my dangerous cycle trips around Shanghai, but many of her friends recognised me and waved from their cars. Perhaps they too felt that it was scarcely worth mentioning. And perhaps my mother was paying me a compliment when she described how I managed to survive at the cliff's edge.

4

My Parents

James Ballard, b. 1902, d. 1967

My father, James Ballard, was born in 1902 and brought up in Blackburn, Lancashire. I never met either of his parents, who died in the 1930s. My father rarely talked about his childhood, and I think that by the time of the Second World War he had separated himself from his Blackburn background, seeing it as part of an exhausted England that he was glad to leave in 1929. He became a much-travelled businessman, a lifelong admirer of the scientific world view and an enthusiast of all things American.

But he remained a Lancashireman to the end, loving tripe, Blackpool and Lancashire comedians. My mother Edna described his own mother as very warm and maternal, and this may have given him the confidence to leave England and see the world. My impression is that family life was prosperous and happy, but he told me once that he had fierce arguments with his father when he left Blackburn Grammar School and

My father, James Ballard, in Shanghai in 1946.

decided to work for a science degree rather than enter the family drapery business. He believed in the power of science to create a better world, and was proud of his first-class honours degree from London University. He was always optimistic and confident, was a great ballroom dancer and even won a prize in a competition held in the Blackpool Tower ballroom.

Most of his memories of Lancashire before and after the

First World War seemed fairly bleak, and he would shake his head as he described the dreadful poverty. Eating an apple as he left school, he was often followed by working-class boys badgering him for the core. He was a strong billiards and bridge player, and was interested in wines and European food. In Shanghai he was almost the only person I knew who was interested in Chinese history and customs. He told me that he once sang solo treble in Manchester cathedral. My impression is that he was a popular and outgoing figure in Blackburn, and later in Shanghai, something that, as an introvert, he achieved by an effort of will.

My father joined the Calico Printers Association, the textile combine that was then the ICI of the cotton world, in the mid 1920s. He had taken his degree in chemistry, the science that had transformed the printing and finishing of textiles, and he often enthused to me about the brilliant work of the great German chemists in the dyestuffs industry. By the 1920s the CPA found that Lancashire cotton could no longer compete in the world's markets with locally produced cotton goods, in particular with the output of the Japanese mills in Shanghai, which dominated the huge China market. The CPA set up an overseas subsidiary in the city, and my father was sent out in 1929 to run its operation there, the China Printing and Finishing Company.

After the war he stayed on in Shanghai, and was present when the Chinese Communists led by Mao Tse-tung seized the city in 1949. Under Chinese supervision he continued to run China Printing, but when the CPA head office in Manchester refused to remit any further funds, my father was put on trial. He told me that he was able to quote numerous passages from Marx and Engels in his defence, and so impressed the Communist peasant judges that they dismissed the charges against him. In 1950, after a long journey across China, he reached Canton, and crossed to Hong Kong.

On returning to England he left the CPA and became a consultant specialising in pharmaceutical textiles. He retired with my mother to the New Forest, and died of cancer in 1967.

Edna Ballard, b. 1905, d. 1999

My mother was born in West Bromwich, near Birmingham, in 1905, and died aged 93 in Claygate, Surrey, in 1999. Her parents, Archibald and Sarah Johnstone, were lifelong teachers of music. During the year that I lived with them, after my mother and sister returned to Shanghai in 1947, two practice pianos were going all day as a series of pupils came and went. When I first met them, in early 1946, after landing in Southampton, they were both in their late sixties, and seemed to be living relics of the Victorian world. With their rigid, intolerant minds, they never relaxed, hating the post-war Labour government, uninterested in my sister or myself, and barely interested in my mother and her wartime

My mother, Edna Ballard, in Shanghai in 1936.

experiences in a Japanese camp. Life was intensely narrow for them, living in a large, three-storey house where the rooms were always dark, filled with heavy, uncomfortable furniture and interior doors with stained-glass panels. Food rationing was in force, but everything seemed to be rationed, the air we breathed, hope of a better world, and the brief glimpses of the sun. Even as a boy I wondered how my mother and her sister, both lively and strong-willed women, had ever managed to bloom as teenage girls.

Yet in later years my mother told me that her father had been something of a rebel in his younger days, and before his marriage had scandalised his family by giving up his musical training and forming a band, which played at dances and weddings. I met him at the worst time, when England was exhausted by the war. There had been heavy bombing in the Birmingham area, and I suspect that they felt my mother's years in Lunghua were a holiday by comparison. The war had made them mean, as it made a lot of the English mean. I think they distrusted me on sight. When my grandmother, a small and ungenerous woman, first showed me the single bathroom in this large, gloomy house I blotted my copybook for ever by asking: 'Is this my bathroom?'

After her death my grandfather went through a remarkable transformation that seems to have begun as he walked away from the funeral. He immediately sold the house and its furniture, and set off with two suitcases for the south coast of England, where he lived in a series of hotels, entirely self-sufficient, moving on if he disliked the menu and facilities. He was living in a Bournemouth hotel when he died at 97. In his last years he would sometimes faint in supermarkets and shops. One manageress, assuming he was dead, rang my mother with the sad news, and was shocked out of her skin when my grandfather, his heart rested, suddenly lifted his head and spoke to her.

My mother rarely talked about her life in West Bromwich,

or the large family of which the Johnstones were part. She never gave me any idea if she was happy or unhappy. The only thing she ever told me about her schooldays was that the future film actress Madeleine Carroll was in the same class at the West Bromwich Grammar School for Girls. For a brief period she worked as a teacher in a junior school in West Bromwich, and was appalled by the dreadful poverty of many of the children.

She and my father met at a holiday hotel in the Lake District, one of the hydros which were very popular with young people in the 1920s. After their marriage, in the later 1920s, when my father had joined the Calico Printers Association, they lived briefly in a rented house in the Manchester area, and sailed for Shanghai in 1929.

My parents never spoke about their reasons for leaving England, and it never occurred to me to ask them. Whether or not they were fully aware of what faced them, they were taking huge risks, not least with their health in a remote, poverty-stricken country long before the era of antibiotics. Cholera, smallpox and typhoid were rife in Shanghai. The piped water was not safe enough to drink – our drinking water was boiled and then stored in the refrigerator in old gin bottles – but all dishes were washed in water straight from the tap. Both my sister and I caught amoebic dysentery and were severely ill. Shanghai was a large and violent city of criminal gangs and murderous political factions. My mother was a 25-year-old newly married woman who had never been out of England, except for a honeymoon trip to Paris. Shanghai was five weeks away by P&O boat. There was no air link, and the only direct contact with England was by cable. I imagine that my father, always determined and optimistic, convinced my mother that England would take years to climb out of the recession, and that far more interesting possibilities waited for them on the other side of the world.

5

The Attack on Pearl Harbor (1941)

The Japanese air attack on Pearl Harbor, the American naval base near Honolulu, took place on the morning of Sunday, 7 December 1941, and brought Japan and America into what was now a world war. In Shanghai, across the International Date Line, it was already Monday, 8 December, and I was lying in bed reading my Bible. This was not for religious reasons – my parents were strongly agnostic. But scripture was my best subject, perhaps because I responded to the strong stories in the classroom versions of the Old Testament. At any rate, I still remember the scornful tones in which the Reverend Matthews announced the winner of a Bible competition. 'First, and the biggest heathen in the class, is Ballard.' A schoolmaster's favourite phrase, no doubt, but I took great pride in it. I remember telling everyone that not only was I an atheist, but I was going to join the Communist Party. I admired anyone who could unsettle people, and the Communist labour organisers had certainly unsettled my father.

I was preparing for the Christmas term exams, and the scripture test was to be held that day. Then I heard what sounded like tanks and military vehicles moving down Amherst Avenue, and my father burst into my bedroom. He stared around wildly, as if he had never seen my room before. He ordered me to get dressed, and told me that Japan had declared war. 'But I have to go to school,' I protested. 'Exams start today.' He then uttered the greatest words a schoolboy can ever hear. 'There'll be no more school, and no more exams.'

I took all this in my stride, but my father was clearly rattled. He raced around the house, shouting at the servants and at my mother. I assume he had heard on the local radio stations that Japanese forces were entering the International Settlement. They swiftly seized control, and their naval units on the Whangpoo river sank the British gunboat, HMS *Petrel*, whose crew put up a spirited fight. Later, Japanese officers visited the wounded survivors in hospital and, out of respect for their courage, bowed to them in the best traditions of bushido. The American gunboat, the USS *Wake*, was captured without a shot being fired – almost all the crew were ashore, asleep with their girlfriends in the hotels of downtown Shanghai.

The French Concession was already under the control of the Vichy government, and the Japanese army seized all key sites within the Settlement. That day their Kempeitai (the Japanese Gestapo) arrested several hundred British and

American civilians, who were the first Allied nationals to be interned. By luck my father was not among them, and we remained in our house until March 1943. Those imprisoned soon after the Pearl Harbor attack were brutally treated, but in Shanghai, fortu-nately, there were a large number of Swiss and Swedish nationals, and their presence may have restrained the Japanese, though there were many violent arrests and killings.

The old Shanghai ceased to exist from this point. There were no more parties or film premieres, no more visits to department stores and the swimming pool. The Country Club became a Japanese officers' club – my mother told me in tones of great indignation that they had stabled their horses in the squash courts. The Japanese army aggressively enforced its presence throughout the Settlement, and street executions of Chinese were common. All foreign cars were confiscated, and my father bought a bicycle to take him the five miles to his office.

The China Printing and Finishing Company still functioned, presumably as a useful source of revenue for the Japanese. There were two Japanese supervisors in the office – one of them was an architect – and I think my father had reasonable relations with them, though he was probably forced to lay off staff. Once when I was with him in his office he took me for a walk around the Cathedral cloisters nearby. Eventually a middle-aged White Russian joined us, and my father handed him some money. He thanked my father profusely and slipped away. As firms and factories closed, jobs must have been difficult to find. The Russian seemed desperately poor, and my father told me matter-of-factly that the shirt and collar beneath his tie and waistcoat was a tiny bib stitched together from rags, which he washed every day in the river.

Social life in the British community came to an end, along with my mother's bridge and tennis parties. Except for the chauffeur, who was rehired after the war, we employed the same number of servants, including the latest in the line of Russian nannies, and they stayed with us until a few days before we were interned.

My parents spent hours listening to the short-wave radio broadcasts from Britain and America. The fall of Singapore, and the sinking of the British battleships *Repulse* and *Prince of Wales*, devastated us all. British prestige plummeted from that moment. The surrender of Singapore, the capture of the Philippines and the threat to India and Australia sounded the death knell of Western power in the Far East and the end of a way of life. It would take the British years to recover from Dunkirk, and the German armies were already deep inside Russia. Despite my admiration for the Japanese soldiers and pilots, I was intensely patriotic, but I could see that the British Empire had failed. I began to look at A.A. Milne and the *Chums* annuals with a far more sceptical eye.

Yet I remember, some time in 1942, my father pinning a large map of Russia to the wall near the radio, and marking out the shifting front line between the Germans and Russians. In many areas the Germans were in retreat, though the Russian front advanced with agonising slowness, a village at a time. All the same, my father had begun to recover a little of his confidence.

I constantly asked him how long the war would last and I remember that he was convinced it would go on for several years. Here he was at odds with many of the English in Shanghai, who still believed that the defeated British forces in the Far East would rally and swiftly defeat the Japanese. Even I, at the age of 11 or 12, knew that this was a dangerous delusion. I had seen the Japanese soldiers at close quarters, and knew that they were tougher, more disciplined and far better led than the British and American soldiers in Shanghai, who seemed bored and only interested in going home. But many of the fathers of boys in my form still assumed that the war would be over in a few months.

My one great disappointment was that the Cathedral School reopened, within a month or so of Pearl Harbor. I cycled to school, but always came straight home afterwards, though sometimes I had to wait for hours to get through the checkpoint at the end of the Avenue Joffre. Downtown Shanghai was far too dangerous, as Japanese military vehicles swerved through the streets, knocking rickshaws and cyclists out of their way, and Chinese puppet troops harassed any Europeans who caught their eye.

Despite these hazards, my father insisted that I attend

school. One morning we cycled together to the Avenue Joffre checkpoint and found that it had been closed as part of a military sweep, along with all other checkpoints into the International Settlement. Undeterred, my father wheeled his bicycle through the crowd and set off with me along the Columbia Road to the house of English friends. Their long garden ended at the barbed-wire fence first erected around the Settlement in 1937 and now in disrepair. Helped by the English friends, we lifted our cycles through the loosened wire and stepped into the grounds of a derelict casino and nightclub named the Del Monte. Concerned that there might be Japanese in the building, my father told me to wait while he stepped through an open rear door. After a few minutes I could no longer restrain myself, and walked on tiptoe through the silent gaming rooms where roulette tables lay on their sides and the floor was covered with broken glasses and betting chips. Gilded statues propped up the canopy of the bars that ran the length of the casino, and on the floor ornate chandeliers cut down from the ceiling tilted among the debris of bottles and old newspapers. Everywhere gold glimmered in the half-light, transforming this derelict casino into a magical cavern from the *Arabian Nights* tales. But it held a deeper meaning for me, the sense that reality itself was a stage set that could be dismantled at any moment, and that no matter how magnificent anything appeared, it could be swept aside into the debris of the past.

I also felt that the ruined casino, like the city and the world beyond it, was more real and more meaningful than it had been when it was thronged with gamblers and dancers. Abandoned houses and office buildings held a special magic and on my way home from school I often paused outside an empty apartment block. Seeing everything displaced and rearranged in a haphazard way gave me my first taste of the surrealism of everyday life, though Shanghai was already surrealist enough.

Then my father appeared through the shadows and led the way to the rear door. We parted at the ramshackle gates of the casino, and he cycled off to his office while I rode the few hundred yards to the Cathedral School and another day of Latin unseens.

Stranger days arrived in early 1943 when full-scale internment began, and British, Belgian and Dutch civilians were moved to the half-dozen camps that now ringed Shanghai. Lunghua Civilian Assembly Centre, in the open countryside five miles to the south, occupied a former training college for Chinese teachers, but several of the smaller camps were in the Shanghai suburbs. Private estates of some forty or fifty houses (today's gated communities) sharing a perimeter wall and a guarded entrance were a popular feature in 1930s Shanghai, and were generally occupied by a single nationality. There was a German estate on Amherst Avenue, an intimidating collection of white boxes that I never tried to enter. Naturally, these well-guarded residential estates made ideal internment camps. The security measures that kept intruders out worked just as well at keeping their former residents in. One of these camps, in which the Kendall-Wards were interned, even dispensed with the need for a barbed-wire fence. As it happened, there were few escapes from the camps. The most famous escaper was a British sailor who walked out of the hospital where he was being treated after the sinking of HMS *Petrel* and spent the war with his Russian girlfriend in the French Concession.

Already, though, everything was becoming too uncertain even for a 12-year-old who thrived on change. I went to visit a close friend in the Avenue Joffre and found the door of his family apartment open and unlocked. The family had left at short notice, and discarded suitcases lay across the unmade beds. Curtains swayed in the open windows, as if celebrating their new freedom. I sat for a long time in my friend's bed-room, staring at his toy soldiers and the model aircraft we had played with happily for so many hours.

Preoccupied with myself and the fate of my friends. I probably had no idea of the stress my parents endured as they faced the prospect of internment. Looking back from the vantage point of 2007, it puzzles me that they decided to stay on in Shanghai when they must have known that war was imminent. But the China Printing and Finishing Company was my father's responsibility, and duty then counted for something. Many foreign-owned businesses run by the Swiss and Swedes were still functioning, and my father may have hoped that the demand for cotton goods was so vast that he would be allowed to compete with the Japanese mills in Shanghai. At the same time, it may have seemed inconceivable that the Japanese would launch a pre-emptive attack on the United States, and even try to extend their 'Co-Prosperity Sphere' as far as India and Australia.

As I watched my father putting his coloured pins into the map of Russia, smiling a little wanly as the radio announcer spoke through the static about captured German steam locomotives, I may already have realised that there were limits to how far I could depend on my parents. When two senior officers in the Kempeitai came to our house and strolled around in their highly polished boots, my father watched them without a word, and was only concerned that I and my 4-year-old sister remain silent. The Japanese officers had not come to arrest my father, as he must have assumed, but were checking the facilities that the house offered once we were interned. My father had no answer to them, and I knew that the time might come when my mother and I, and my sister, would be alone. Few middle-class children in times of peace see their parents under severe stress, and I had been brought up to regard my father and his male friends as figures of confidence and authority. Now everything was changing, and a new kind of education had begun. The sight of English adults under stress replaced the Latin unseens.

By the end of 1942 the war in the Pacific began to turn

against the Japanese. Their navy, which had caught the Americans by surprise at Pearl Harbor, suffered catastrophic defeats at the Battles of Midway and the Coral Sea. British resistance was stiffening in Burma, and in Europe there were the beginnings of what would become the heroic Bomber Command offensive against Germany. I wanted to encourage my father, whom I knew to be a thoughtful and brave man, but nothing in his experience had prepared him for the Japanese military with its centuries-old codes of discipline and its demands of absolute submission from any captured enemy.

Given the importance of Shanghai and its huge dockyards, the Japanese decided to intern the British and other Allied nationals. Lunghua Camp was sited in a notorious malaria zone (the Shanghai High School which now occupies the former camp is still plagued by mosquitoes, and in 1991 the British Airways Travel Clinic warned me to leave the area before dusk). My father and other members of the British Residents Association complained strongly to the Japanese authorities in Shanghai, but the construction of Lunghua Camp went ahead.

In March 1943 my parents, sister and I entered Lunghua, where we remained until the end of August 1945.

6

Lunghua Camp (1943)

Our assembly point for the journey to Lunghua was the American Club in Columbia Road, a mile from Amherst Avenue. When we arrived we found a huge press of people, mostly British with a few Belgians and Dutch, sitting with their suitcases around the swimming pool, many of the women in their fur coats. Some of the men carried nothing apart from the clothes they were wearing, still confident that the war would be over within days. Others had strapped tennis rackets, cricket bats and fishing rods to their luggage – we had been told that there were a number of large and very deep ponds within the camp. A few were drunk, aware that they faced long months far from the nearest bar. Together we waited around the swimming pool, sitting at the tables where the American members of the club had once sipped their bourbons and mint juleps. Then the Japanese guards arrived with a small fleet of buses, and we were on our way across the open countryside, among the last group of Allied nationals to be interned.

For an hour we trundled through the deserted country-side, past empty villages and recent battlefields that I remembered from earlier drives with my parents and their friends. We passed the pagoda at Lunghua, where Japanese soldiers were hoisting anti-aircraft guns onto the upper decks. Nearby was a military airfield, Zero fighters lined up in front of the hangars. On all sides there were derelict canals and untended paddy fields, a waterlogged land through which the great arm of the Whangpoo river moved on its way to Shanghai and the sea.

Then Lunghua Camp appeared, my last real childhood home, where I would spend the next two and a half largely happy years. As we drove past sections of brand-new barbed-wire fencing, the camp resembled a half-ruined college campus. There were three-storey concrete buildings, pock-marked by shellfire but still standing. Other buildings were mounds of rubble, cement floors concertinaed together as if after an earthquake. There was a guardhouse by the gates, Japanese soldiers staring at us stonily. There were smaller buildings with pitched roofs of red tile, and rows of freshly built wooden huts, each some fifty yards long. Washing hung everywhere on makeshift lines, but there was a faint smell of sewage on the air, shared with a million mosquitoes.

And then there were the internees. We stepped down from our bus, greeted by a friendly crowd who helped us with our suitcases and guided families with small children towards G Block, a two-storey building that held some forty small

The former F Block in Lunghua Camp, in 1991.

rooms. Our bedding had been sent on ahead, and assembled for us by friends of my father. I remember how he and my mother sat together on one of the beds with my sister, staring at this tiny space, as small as the rooms in the servants' quarters at 31 Amherst Avenue, which had also contained entire families. Keen to greet schoolfriends I had recognised in the crowd around the bus, I left my parents to their new domain and began my exploration of Lunghua Camp.

My first impression was of how relaxed and casual the internees seemed. All this would change, but the people around me were enjoying a ramshackle and rather pleasant holiday. I had known a Shanghai where the men wore suits and ties, but here they were dressed in cotton shorts and shirtsleeves. Many of the younger women, among them the rather formal mothers of boys at school, were in beachwear. There were few Japanese guards around, and most of the camp administration was left to the internees. The dining hall where we assembled for our first meal had the atmosphere of an unsupervised prison, children screaming, the husbands flirting with each other's wives, young men playfully squaring off at each other. Later, still in a daze, I was shown around the camp by schoolfriends. There seemed to be humour, or at least the prison-camp version of drollery, in ample supply – earth and cinder road-tracks named Oxford Street and Piccadilly, the drinking-water stations that boiled our water signposted 'Waterloo' and 'Bubbling Well'. On the observation roof of F Block a group of music lovers listened to a classical symphony on a wind-up gramophone. On the steps of the assembly hall the Lunghua Players rehearsed a scene from *The Pirates of Penzance*, though what the young Japanese soldiers in the front row on the opening night actually made of it I can't imagine.

All in all, this was a relaxed and easy-going world that I had never known, except during our holidays in Tsingtao, and this favourable first impression stayed with me to the end, when conditions in the camp took a marked turn for the worse. I enjoyed my years in Lunghua, made a huge number of friends of all ages (far more than I did in adult life) and on the whole felt buoyant and optimistic, even when the food rations fell to near zero, skin infections covered my legs, malnutrition had prolapsed my rectum, and many of the adults had lost heart.

But all that was two years away, and in the spring of 1943 I was happy to make the most of my new world. My parents were glad to let me stay out to all hours, and I set about exploring every corner of the camp, meeting a host of quirky, bored, pleasant and unpleasant characters.

E Block and F Block, the two largest buildings in the former teacher-training college, contained its classrooms, and these were occupied by single internees and married couples without children. Families with children were housed in D and G Blocks, in the rooms that once housed the Chinese student teachers. There was a shower block, which in the first months supplied hot water, a small 'hospital' where my sister was treated for dysentery, and a number of bungalows that had housed the college's senior staff and were the quarters of the Japanese guards.

The camp lay over a substantial area, perhaps half a mile in diameter, ringed by a barbed-wire fence through which I often climbed to retrieve a ball or kite. Japanese soldiers patrolled the wire in a rather casual way, and once I had to hide in the long grass outside the fence when I was searching for a lost baseball and the other children warned me that the guards were approaching. About a third of the original site was excluded from the camp, and contained a number of derelict buildings. With the agreement of the camp commandant, a former diplomat named Hyashi, who had spent time at the London embassy and spoke fluent English, one of these buildings became the camp school. Each day the gates were opened to allow the children to and fro, and we entered the rather eerie world beyond the camp.

There were many open spaces in Lunghua, uncultivated ground littered with stones and war rubble from the fierce fighting that had taken place in and around the buildings of the training college. Over the next year, as our rations fell, groups of internees began to clear the ground and cultivate modest vegetable plots. I helped my father to hoist buckets of sewage from the G Block septic tank, which we used to fertilise our tomatoes, melons and runner beans, though the results of all this labour seemed strangely puny and stunted.

For all the open spaces that surrounded the buildings in the camp, including the assembly ground where football matches were played, inside the crowded dormitories there was a desperate competition for space. In E and F Blocks, the former classrooms that housed married couples were divided into a maze of cubicles by sheets hung from lines of string and rope. Pieces of cardboard, sections of wooden packing cases and anything else to hand helped to provide a minimum of privacy. Within the small family rooms of D and G Blocks the parents had no defence against the children who shared their tiny spaces, and no doubt this explains why my mother and father were happy to let me roam around the camp for as long as I wanted. In many ways the camp became my new Shanghai, with a thousand sights to be investigated and savoured, a hundred errands to be run in return for an old copy of *Life* or an unwanted screwdriver.

All men in the camp were assigned jobs – running the kitchens, unloading the supplies of food and coal trucked into Lunghua from Shanghai, boiling our drinking water, maintaining the electricity supply, teaching the children and conducting religious services. Single women helped wherever they could, nursing and caring for malaria victims. Married women with small children were excused duties of any kind, and my mother rarely left G Block and the tiny room that became our home. During the day my father raised his mattress against the wall, and in the small space we set up a card table at which we ate our meals. Much of the time my mother remained in our room, reading by the window as she kept an eye on my sister playing in the yard outside with the other toddlers.

Families with only a single child were obliged to take in one of the children separated from their parents and interned alone. In G Block a boy named Bobby Henderson was so resented by the couple on whom he was billeted that he constructed a cubicle like a beggar's hovel around his narrow bed. This was his private world that he defended fiercely. He was dressed in cast-offs, and saved his shoes for the winter months. In the summers he wore a pair of wooden clogs with the heels completely worn away, leaving two slivers of wood that ended in his insteps.

Bobby was a close friend, though I never really liked him, and found something threatening about his tough and self-reliant mind. I sensed that circumstances had forced him to fight too hard to survive, and that this had made him ruthless not only with others, but with himself. He allowed me to tag along with him, but regarded my endless curiosity and roaming around the camp as a waste of time and energy, and my interest in chess, bridge and kite building, and in the complex skipping games that some of the girls brought into camp with them, as frivolous and distracting. His parents were interned in Peking, but he never spoke about them, which baffled me at the time, and I suspect that he had forgotten what they were like. Thinking of him now, I realise that part of him had died, and I hope that he never went on to have children of his own.

On the whole, however, Lunghua seemed full of easy-going and agreeable characters. What I liked most was that everyone, of almost any age, could talk to anyone else. Striding around E Block or the assembly hall with my chessboard, I would be affably hailed as 'Shanghai Jim' (for constantly telling anyone who would listen about some strange Hardoon temple I had found on my cycle rides). I would then settle down to a game of chess with a man of my father's age who might be an architect or cinema manager, Cathay Hotel bartender or a former jockey. At the end of the game, which generally involved the transfer from my opponent of a goodly amount of internment camp wisdom,

I might be lent an old copy of the *Saturday Evening Post*, which I understood, or *Punch*, with its incomprehensible humour that my tired mother would have to explain.

During the first year a host of camp activities took place – amateur dramatics, with full-scale performances in the dining hall of Noël Coward and Shakespeare plays, light-hearted revues ('We're the Lunghua sophomores, we're the girls every boy adores, CAC don't mean a thing to me, for every Tuesday evening we go on a spree...'). I forget what happened on Tuesday evenings, and there may have been dances from which all children were excluded. CAC stood for 'Civilian Assembly Centre', an exalted term for our collection of run-down and half-ruined buildings.

Generally I would be somewhere in the audience, fascinated by a lecture on Roman roads or airship design. My father once delivered a lecture on 'Science and the Idea of God', a tactful dismissal of the Almighty from human affairs, which drew many of the English missionaries in the camp. Until the day we left Lunghua I was frequently stopped by one or other of the up-country parsons and told what an excellent lecture it was, so *interesting*, and I wonder if any of them or their high-minded wives had seen the point.

Since there were so many professionally trained men in the camp – engineers, architects, bankers, industrial chemists, dentists and doctors – there was no shortage of lecturers. And, alas, no shortage of teachers for the camp school that soon opened. A full-scale syllabus was set out, which met the requirements of the then School Certificate, and we were taught maths, French, English and Latin, history and general science. Since there were few books our tuition was largely blackboard-driven, but I don't think that any of us fell behind our counterparts at school in wartime England, and in some cases we were well ahead. I find it difficult to explain this, but my guess is that there were far fewer distractions in Lunghua than I imagined at the time, for either teachers or pupils, and that we progressed rapidly in the way that long-term convicted prisoners pass one university degree after another.

Lunghua Camp held some 2000 internees, of whom 300 were children. Most of them were British, Dutch and Belgian, but there was a group of thirty American merchant seamen, captured on board an American freighter. As civilians, they were not sent to a POW camp, and must have realised their good luck. They passed their time loafing on their beds in E Block, though now and then they would rouse themselves and amble out to the assembly ground for a game of softball. I liked them immensely, for their good humour, verbal inventiveness and enormously laid-back style. Life in their company was always interesting, and they remained cheerful to the end, unlike many of the British internees. They always seemed glad to see me, throwing back the curtains of their miniature cubicles, and would go to elaborate lengths to make me the butt of friendly practical jokes, which I took in good part. Among their other virtues, the Americans had a substantial stock of magazines – *Life*, *Time*, *Popular Mechanics*, *Collier's* – which I devoured, desperate for the kind of hard information on which my imagination fed.

What was happening, without my realising it at the time, was that I was meeting a range of adults from whom my life in Shanghai had screened me. This was nothing to do with class in the English sense, but with the fact that pre-war Shanghai attracted to its bars and hotel lobbies a number of devious and unscrupulous characters who were very good company, and often far more generous with a sweet potato than the tight-fisted Church of England missionaries. Many of these 'rogues', as my mother termed them, had well-stocked minds (perhaps based on their extensive prison-cell reading in England) and could come up with arresting ideas about everything under the sun. Years of property and financial scams, of rigged bets at jai alai games and the Shanghai racecourse, had added salt to their easy wit. I hung on every word, and even tried to model myself on them, without success. When I first tried 'the university of life' on my mother she stared at me without speaking for a full minute.

But I loved hearing adults talk together. I would sidle up unnoticed to a group of G Block adults discussing the servant problem in Shanghai, their last leaves in Hong Kong or Singapore, the refusal by some fellow internee to do his share of the lavatory-cleaning fatigue, pre-war gossip about Mrs

So-and-so, until they noticed my keen ears and gleaming eyes and ordered me to hop it.

What all these adults shared, of which I took full advantage, was the crushing boredom of camp life. The war was far away and the news we received, percolating through delivery drivers and Red Cross visits, was months late. The Lunghua internees were living in an eventless world, with little to distract them other than the sound of a few Japanese planes taking off from the nearby airfield. An hour's chess with a talkative 12-year-old was an hour less to endure, and even a discussion about the relative merits of the Packard and the Rolls-Royce could help the afternoon along.

The adults in the camp were also coming to terms with the most significant change in their lives, almost on a par with the war itself, and one which histories of internment often overlook – the absence of alcohol. After years and sometimes decades of heavy drinking (the core of social and professional life in the 1930s), Lunghua Camp must have functioned for its first months as a highly efficient health spa. One serious hazard still remained: malaria. The Lunghua area, with its stagnant paddy fields and canals, was notorious for its malaria, though luckily the Ballard family was immune. My mother later claimed that 50 per cent of the internees caught malaria. This sounds high to me, but I have seen official post-war estimates of 30 per cent.

Our food supply was a serious problem from the start. Hungry children will eat anything, but my parents must have shuddered at the thought of another day's meals. At no time during the years of internment did we see milk, butter, margarine, eggs or sugar. Our meals consisted of rice congee (rice boiled into a liquid pulp), vegetable soup that concealed one or two dice-sized pieces of gristly horse meat, a hard black bread baked from what must have been godown sweepings and filled with bits of rusty wire and stony grit, and grey sweet potatoes, a cattle feed that I adored. Later there was a cereal called cracked wheat, another cattle feed that I took a great liking to. Somehow my parents and the other adults forced this down, but I always had a strong appetite, and to this day I find it difficult to leave food on my plate, even if I dislike its taste.

In the last eighteen months of the war our rations fell steeply. As we sat at the card table in our room one day, pushing what my mother called 'the weevils' to the rim of our plates of congee, my father decided that from then on we should eat the weevils – we needed the protein. They were small white slugs, and perhaps were maggots, a word my mother preferred to avoid. It must have irritated my parents when I regularly counted them before tucking in lustily – a hundred or so was my usual score, forming a double perimeter around my plate and visibly reducing my portion of boiled rice.

A close friend of my father was a senior Shell executive called Braidwood, who was chairman of the internees committee that ran the camp administration. In the 1980s his widow sent me the typed minutes of the committee meetings, some of which my father attended. These describe a wide range of daily problems and there are copies of formal letters addressed to the Japanese commandant and the military officers who replaced him. They cover the general health of the internees, abusive behaviour by the guards, the lack of medicines, the scarcity of fuel for the drinking-water boilers, the need for Red Cross supplies of clothing (much of which was pilfered by the guards) and, above all, the inadequate food rations – all problems in which the Japanese military had not the slightest interest. According to Braidwood's records, the daily calorie count in 1944 was approximately 1500, and fell sharply to 1300 during 1945. I can only guess what fraction of that figure was represented by the weevils.

7

Chess, Boredom and a Certain Estrangement (1943)

I thrived in Lunghua, and made the most of my years there, in the school report parlance of my childhood. My impression is that, during the first year of internment, life in the camp was tolerable for my parents and most of the other adults. There were very few rows between the internees, despite the cramped space, malaria mosquitoes and meagre rations. Children went regularly to school, and there were packed programmes of sporting and social events, language classes and lectures. All this may have been a necessary illusion, but for a while it worked, and sustained everyone's morale.

Hopes were still high that the war would soon be over, and by the end of 1943 the eventual defeat of Germany seemed almost certain. The commandant, Hyashi, was a civilised man who did his best to meet the internees' demands. Almost a caricature short-sighted Japanese with a toothbrush moustache, spectacles and slightly popping eyes, he would cycle around Lunghua on a tandem bicycle with his small son, also in glasses, sitting on the rear saddle. He would smile at the noisy British children, a feral tribe if there was one, and struck up close relationships with members of the camp committee. Among the documents Mrs Braidwood sent me was a letter which Hyashi wrote to her husband some time after he had been dismissed as commandant, in which he describes (in English) his horse rides around Shanghai and sends his warm regards. After the war my father flew down to the war-crimes trials in Hong Kong and testified as a witness for Hyashi, who was later acquitted and released.

I also made friendships of a kind with several of the young Japanese guards. When they were off duty I would visit them in the staff bungalows fifty yards from G Block, and they would allow me to sit in their hot tubs and then wear their kendo armour. After handing me a duelling sword, a fearsome weapon of long wooden segments loosely strung together, they would encourage me to fence with them. Each bout would last twenty seconds and involved me being repeatedly struck about the helmet and face mask, which I could scarcely see through, every dizzying blow being greeted with friendly cheers from the watching Japanese. They too were bored, only a few years older than me, and had little hope of seeing their families again soon, if ever. I knew they could be viciously brutal, especially when acting under the orders of their NCOs, but individually they were easy-going and likeable. Their military formality and never-surrender ethos were of course very impressive to a 13-year-old looking for heroes to worship.

For me, the most important consequence of internment was that for the first time in my life I was extremely close to my parents. I slept, ate, read, dressed and undressed within a few feet of them in the same small room, in many ways like the poorer Chinese families for whom I had felt so sorry in Shanghai. But I revelled in this closeness, which I assume has been a central part of human behaviour throughout most of its evolution. Lying in bed at night I could, if I wanted to, reach out and take my mother's hand, though I never did. In the early days when there was still electric power my mother would read late into the night, hidden inside her mosquito net only a few feet away, as my father and sister slept in their beds behind us. One night a passing Japanese officer spotted the light through the home-made blackout curtain. He burst into the room, barely a foot from me, drew his sword and slashed away the mosquito net above my mother's head, then thrashed the light bulb into fragments and vanished without a word. I remember the strange silence of people woken in the nearby rooms, listening to his footsteps as he disappeared into the night.

Somehow my mother survived, but she and my father struck up few close friendships with the other G Block internees. Though all had children, the families kept their distance from each other, presumably to maintain their privacy, a desperately short commodity when an evening curfew was introduced and we were confined to quarters for the hours of darkness.

But I flourished in all this intimacy, and I think the years together in that very small room had a profound effect on me and the way I brought up my own children. Perhaps the reason why I have lived in the same Shepperton house for nearly fifty years, and to the despair of everyone have always preferred make-do-and-mend to buying anew, even when I could easily afford it, is that my small and untidy house reminds me of our family room in Lunghua.

I realise now just how formal English life could be in the 1930s, 40s and 50s for its professional families. The children of doctors, lawyers and company directors rarely saw their fathers. They lived in large houses where no one shared a bedroom, they never saw their parents dressing or undressing, never saw them brush their teeth or even take off a watch. In pre-war Shanghai I would occasionally wander into my parents' bedroom and see my mother brushing her hair, a strange and almost mysterious event. I rarely saw my father without a jacket and tie well into the 1950s. The vistas of polished furniture turned a family home into a deserted museum, with a few partly colonised rooms where people slept alone, read and bathed alone, and hung their clothes in private wardrobes, along with their emotions, hopes and dreams.

Lunghua Camp may have been a prison of a kind, but it was a prison where I found freedom. My parents were always at hand to answer any query that crossed my mind – a difficulty with my French prep, the existence or otherwise of God, or the meaning of 'you play on my mistakes', a phrase uttered sagely by my adult chess opponents when they were on the point of losing. In no sense did I think of myself as a misfit (which was certainly true once I came to England in 1946), and nor did anyone else, as far as I can remember. In many ways I was the opposite of a misfit, and adapted too well to the camp. One of my chess partners, a likeable architect named Cummings with a haemophiliac son who became a huge success in Hong Kong after the war, once remarked: 'Jamie, you'll miss Lunghua when you leave…'

Until I arrived in England I had been lucky to have a happy childhood, and any shocks that shaped my character came not from my family but from the outside world – the sudden scene-shifting I witnessed in 1937 and 1941. If anything, the years in Lunghua offered the first stability I had known since I had been a small child, a stability that the adult internees around me had done little or nothing to create. I felt fairly sceptical about the adult world and the notions of good sense and decisive thought promoted by my parents and teachers. War, I knew, was an irrational business, and the sensible predictions of architects, doctors and managing directors had a marked tendency to be wrong.

I have given a general picture of Lunghua Camp in my

novel *Empire of the Sun,* which is partly autobiographical and partly fictional, though many incidents are described as they occurred. At the same time, I accept that the novel is based on the memories of a teenage boy, who responded more warmly to the good cheer of the American sailors than to the rather torpid Brits, many of whom had held modest jobs in Shanghai and probably regretted ever leaving England.

In my novel the most important break with real events is the absence from Lunghua of my parents. I thought hard about this, but I felt that it was closer to the psychological and emotional truth of events to make 'Jim' effectively a war orphan. There is no doubt that a gradual estrangement from my parents, which lasted to the end of their lives, began in Lunghua Camp. There was never any friction or antagonism, and they did their best to look after me and my sister. Despite the food shortages in the last year, the bitterly cold winters (we lived in unheated concrete buildlings) and the uncertainties of the future, I was happier in the camp than I was until my marriage and children.

At the same time I felt slightly apart from my parents by the time the war ended. One reason for our estrangement was that their parenting became passive rather than active – they had none of the usual levers to pull, no presents or treats, no say in what we ate, no power over how we lived or ability to shape events. Like all the adults, they were nervous of the highly unpredictable Japanese and Korean guards, they were often unwell, and always short of food and clothing. At one point, when my shoes had fallen to tatters, my father gave me a pair of heavy leather golfing shoes with metal studs, but the sound of me stamping down the stone corridors in G Block brought the internees swiftly to attention outside their doors, assuming that the Japanese had called a sudden inspection. I would find myself desperately trying to get to the Ballard room before anyone noticed who was actually inspecting them. Needless to say, I soon had to return the shoes to my father, and G Block was able to relax.

Thoughts of food filled every hour, as they did for the other teenage boys in Lunghua. I don't remember my parents ever giving me their own food, and I'm sure that no other parents shared their rations with their children. All mothers, in prison camps or famine regions, know that their own health is vital to the survival of their children. A child who has lost its parent is in desperate danger, and the parents in Lunghua must have realised that they needed all the strength they had for the uncertain years ahead. But I scavenged what I could, stealing tomatoes and cucumbers from any unwatched vegetable plot. The camp was, in effect, a huge slum, and in any slum it is the teenage boys who run wild. I have never looked down on the helpless parents in sink housing estates unable to control their children. I remember my own parents in the camp, unable to warn, chide, praise or promise.

All the same I regret the estrangement, and realise how much I have missed. The experience of seeing adults under stress is an education in itself, but bought, sadly, at too heavy a price. When my mother, sister and I sailed for England at the end of 1945 my father remained in Shanghai, returning for a brief visit to England in 1947, when we toured Europe in his large American car. I was 17, about to go to Cambridge, unsure whether to be a doctor or a writer. My father was a friendly but already distant figure who played no part in my decision. When he returned for good in 1950 he had been away from England for more than twenty years, and the advice he gave me about English life was out of date. I went my own way, ignoring him when he strongly urged me against becoming a writer. I had spent five years learning to decode the strange, introverted world of English life, while he was happiest dealing with his professional colleagues in Switzerland and America. He telephoned to congratulate me on my first novel, *The Drowned World*, pointing out one or two minor errors that I was careful not to correct. My mother never showed the slightest interest in my career until *Empire of the Sun*, which she thought was about her.

As an itinerant chess player and magazine hunter, I got to know a huge number of Lunghua internees, but few reappeared in my later life. One was the headmaster of the camp school, a Methodist missionary called George

Osborne. Knowing of my father's strongly agnostic and pro-scientific beliefs, he generously urged him to send me to his old school, The Leys in Cambridge, founded by well-to-do Methodists from the north of England and very much science-oriented. Osborne was an unworldly figure, blinking through his glasses and tireless in his efforts to keep the camp together, and the best kind of practising Christian. His wife and three children were in England, but once the war ended his first thoughts were for his Chinese flock at their upcountry mission station, to which he returned rather than sail home. After a year there he paid a brief visit to England, taking me out to lunch whenever he was in Cambridge. By chance, in the 1960s, I became close friends with a north London doctor, Martin Bax, who edited a poetry magazine with his wife Judy. A decade later I learned that Judy Bax was the Reverend Osborne's daughter. As she admitted, I knew her father far more closely than she did.

Another Lunghua acquaintance was Cyril Goldbert, the future Peter Wyngarde. Separated from his parents, he lived with another family in G Block, and amused everyone with his fey and extravagant manner. Theatre was his entire world, and he played adult roles in the camp Shakespeare productions, completely dominating the bank managers and company directors who struggled to keep up with him. He was four years older than me, and very witty company, with a sophisticated patter I had rarely come across. He had never been to England, but seemed to be on first-name terms with half of Shaftesbury Avenue, and was a mine of insider gossip about the London theatre.

Cyril was very popular with the ladies, distributing the most gallant flattery, and my mother always remembered him with affection. 'Oh, Cyril...' she would chortle when she saw him on television in the 1960s. Throughout her life my mother had an active dislike of homosexuals, understandable perhaps at a time when a conviction for homosexual acts brought not just the prison cell but social disgrace. Every married woman's deep fear must have been that husband, breadwinner and father of her children might have a secret self in a carefully locked closet. When I was in my late teens she saw me reading a collection of Oscar Wilde's plays, and literally prised the volume from my hands, although I was already showing a keen interest in girls of my age.

I once strolled with Cyril through some ruined buildings on the outskirts of the camp, listening to him set out his plans for his conquest of the West End. He tore a piece of charcoal from a burnt roof beam, and with a flourish drew on the wall what he said would be his stage name once he returned to England: Laurence Templeton. A name wonderfully of its time, and far grander than Peter Wyngarde. I met him in the early fifties in the Mitre pub in Holland Park Avenue in London, and he was in a poor way, with bad teeth and tired eyes. But ten years later he achieved huge success, not on stage but on television, as Jason King. I saw him in St

James's Park, camel-hair coat stylishly slung over an elegant suit, a tilted homburg and dazzling teeth. I started to speak to him but he cut me dead.

8

American Air Raids (1944)

My parents' memories of Lunghua were always much harsher than my own. I was often hungry, but I revelled in camp life, roaming everywhere, at the centre of a pack of boys my own age, playing chess with bored internees in the men's huts and quizzing them between moves about the world. At the same time I knew nothing about the progress of the war, and our likely fate at the hands of the Japanese.

Occasional Red Cross supplies kept us going, but the adults must have been weak and demoralised, with no end in sight to the war. Many years later, my mother told me that in 1944 there were strong rumours relayed from the Swiss neutrals in Shanghai that the Japanese high command planned to close the camp and march us all up-country, where they would dispose of us. The Japanese armies in China, millions strong, were falling back to the coast, and intended to make their last stand near the mouth of the Yangtze against the expected American landings. This must have deeply alarmed my parents and other adults in the know, however uncertain the rumours.

Unaware of all this, I went on wheedling tattered copies of *Life* and *Popular Mechanics* from the American sailors in E Block, setting pheasant traps (we never caught a bird) and flirting with the skinny but attractive teenage girls in G Block who had grown into puberty with me. Fortunately the Hiroshima and Nagasaki A-bombs brought the war to an abrupt end. Like my parents, and everyone else who lived through Lunghua, I have long supported the American dropping of the bombs. Prompted by Emperor Hirohito's surrender broadcast, the still-intact Japanese war machine ground to a complete halt within days, so saving millions of Chinese lives, as well as our own. For a hint of what might otherwise have happened, we can look at the vicious battle for Manila, the only large city in the Pacific War fought for by the Americans, where some 100,000 Philippine civilians died.

By the summer of 1944 the conditions in Lunghua Camp had changed markedly for the worse. Japanese forces in the Pacific were falling back under fierce attacks by American air and naval power, and US submarines were taking a heavy toll of Japanese shipping to and from the home islands. Japanese cities were one by one being devastated by American bombers. The Tokyo high command could barely feed its own soldiers, let alone the groups of civilian internees scattered throughout the Far East.

The behaviour of the Japanese guards in Lunghua became more brutal as Japan faced defeat. Far from wanting to ingratiate themselves, the guards would lash out at the male internees during the roll-calls. The Japanese soldiers making up the original force of guards were replaced by older recruits, and then by Korean conscripts who had themselves been brutalised by the Japanese NCOs, and were particularly vicious.

After the war we learned that throughout our internment there had been three clandestine radios in the camp, and that an inner group of internees were closely following the progress of the war. Sensibly, they kept their news to themselves, for fear that the few collaborators in the camp would tip off the guards. A married Englishwoman in G Block spoke fluent Japanese and worked in the commandant's office, and she was widely suspected of passing on information to the Japanese, knowingly or otherwise, perhaps in return for medicines for her sick son.

I assume that she knew nothing about the camp radios, but the encouraging news about the war may have prompted the first escape from the camp in 1944. A group of five or six men stepped through the wire and set off for the Chinese lines 400 miles away, and they were followed by others. One group made it to freedom, but others were betrayed by Chinese villagers terrified of ferocious reprisals from the Japanese.

An immediate result was the sacking of the camp

commandant, Hyashi. Lunghua was placed under the direct command of the Japanese military, and a harsher regime followed. The food ration was cut, and a second inner barbed-wire fence was built around the central cluster of buildings that housed the unmarried internees. The gates were shut at 7 o'clock, which meant that G Block was cut off from much of camp life in the evenings. Presumably the Japanese decided that married men with children were not likely to escape. Roll-calls were stepped up, and took place twice daily, when we stood wearily in the corridor outside our rooms as the guards laboriously checked that we were all present. Whenever there was a major infraction of camp regulations, or a significant defeat of their forces in the Pacific, the new commandant would impose a curfew and close the camp school, sometimes for two or three days, a real punishment for the parents forced to endure their fractious children.

The shower block was closed, and from then on we had to carry buckets of warm water from the Bubbling Well and Waterloo heating stations, an exhausting daily chore that I performed for my mother (my father was working as a stoker in the camp kitchens). The two dining halls were also closed, and food arrived on metal-wheeled carts pulled by two of the G Block internees. As ravenous as ever, I would listen out for the metal creaking of the cartwheels, and then rush to be first in the queue as our ration of congee and sweet potato was doled out in the entrance hall. Later, while everyone recovered from their meal, I would help push the cart back to the kitchens and be allowed to scrape the bottom of the potato bin.

Lunghua winters were fiercely cold. We were living in unheated buildings, and many people retired to bed for as long as they could. My father learned from George Osborne that many of the windows in the school classrooms had lost their glass during the 1937 battles around Lunghua. Somehow my father persuaded parents to contribute whatever old pieces of cloth they had kept. He cut these into dozens of small squares, melted candles into a shallow tray and soaked the cotton in the molten wax. Tacked into place by the teachers, they kept much of the icy wind from our classrooms.

My mother liked to brew tea to keep warm, and one of my chess opponents, a garage owner named Richards, taught me how to build a chatty, a primitive Chinese stove constructed from a five-gallon oilcan that we pilfered from the guards' refuse tip. We gouged reinforcing bars from the flaking concrete of the ruined buildings, slotted them through the can above a draught door and then moulded wet clay to form a venturi. The kitchen ovens burned a low-grade coking coal, and in the tips outside the furnaces one could find small pieces of coke. I squatted on the still-warm ash-tips, poking with a bent piece of wire through the dust and clinkers, and thinking of the Chinese beggar boys who picked over the Avenue Joffre ash-tips. I remember reflecting on this without comment, and I make no comment now.

My father sometimes brought small portions of boiled rice for my mother, but as a principled man refused to bring any coal to fuel the chatty. In my roamings around the camp I found a broken Chinese bayonet, a handle and three inches of snapped blade. Over a few weeks I sharpened this to a point, rubbing away at any hard stone I could find. One evening, in the darkness an hour before curfew, I led Bobby Henderson to the rear wall of the coal store behind the kitchens, and used the bayonet to scrape away the mortar. After removing two of the bricks, I drew out several handfuls of coal, which I divided between us, then replaced the bricks in the wall.

My father said nothing when I showed him the coal, though he must have known that I had stolen it from the kitchen storeroom. I soon had it glowing brightly in the chatty outside the rear entrance to G Block, and my father carried a warming cup of black tea to my bedridden mother. Both of us knew that he had compromised his principles, but at the same time I felt that I had gained no merit in his eyes. I take it for granted that if the war had continued for much longer the sense of community and the social constraints that held the internees together would have broken down. Moral principles, along with kindness and generosity, are worth less than they might seem. At the time, as the glowing coals warmed my hands, I wondered what Henderson would do with his share of the coal. Later I saw him in the darkness, hurling the pieces into the deep pond beyond the perimeter fence.

In late 1944 conditions in Lunghua continued to worsen, not through deliberate neglect by the Japanese authorities, but because they had lost all interest in us. The food supply fell, and the internees' health was eroded by malaria, exhaustion and a general resignation to further years of war. The Americans had advanced island by island across the Pacific, but they were still hundreds of miles away. The huge Japanese armies in China were ready to defend the Emperor and the home islands to the last man.

Nowhere had Japanese soldiers surrendered in large numbers. Fatalism, fierce discipline and a profound patriotism shaped their warrior spirit. In some way, I think, the Japanese soldier assumed unconsciously that he had already died in battle, and the apparent life left to him was on a very short lease. This explained their vicious cruelty. I can still see two of the guards beating to death an exhausted Chinese rickshaw coolie who had brought them from Shanghai. As the desperate man sobbed on his knees the Japanese first kicked his rickshaw to pieces, probably his only possession in the world and sole source of income, and then began to beat and kick the Chinese until he lay in a still and bloody pulp on the ground.

All this took place some thirty feet from me by the rear

entrance of G Block, and was watched by a large crowd of internees. None of the men spoke, as if their silent stares would force the two Japanese to end their torment. I knew that this was a naive hope, but I also understood why none of the British, all of whom had wives and children, had tried to intervene. The reprisals would have been instant and fearsome. I remember feeling a deep deadness, which may have been noticed by one of my father's friends, who steered me away.

I think that by this time, early 1945, I was already (aged 14!) starting to worry about the future of Lunghua. I realised that the state of Japanese morale was more important than that of the internees, and I was glad to see the Japanese guards helping the internee working parties to repair the main gates of the camp and keep out the destitute Chinese peasants who had crossed the stricken countryside and were hoping to find sanctuary in Lunghua. Starving families sat around the gates, the women wailing and holding up their skeletal children, like the beggars who had clustered outside the office buildings of downtown Shanghai. If the Japanese abandoned Lunghua we would be exposed to roaming groups of militia soldiers, little more than bandits, and to units of the former puppet armies left to fend for themselves, all armed and eager to ransack the camp.

I kept careful watch on the barbed-wire fence, and turned my back on the younger children still playing the traditional games that I forgot when I came to England and sadly never passed on to my own children – marbles and hopscotch, and complicated skipping and ball games. I had read the camp's entire stock of magazines several times over, but I still visited the American seamen. Cheerful as ever, they were obsessed with their pheasant traps, which I helped them lay in the open ground between E Block and the perimeter fence. I suspect now that they were really marking out an escape route beyond the eyes of the Japanese, in the event of a major emergency like the sudden closure of the camp.

The first American air raids over Shanghai had begun in the summer of 1944, and steadily intensified over the following months. High-flying reconnaissance planes appeared in the sky, strangely motionless as they hung between the clouds. Soon after, squadrons of fighters, Mustangs and twin-engined Lightnings, flew in from the south to attack Lunghua airfield. As they approached, barely twenty feet above the abandoned paddy fields, they hid behind the three-storey buildings of Lunghua Camp, then swerved away to strafe the parked Japanese planes and nearby hangars. Lunghua pagoda had been turned into a flak tower by the Japanese, and as I watched the attacks from the first-floor balcony of the men's washroom the pagoda was lit up like a Christmas tree, gunfire flickering from its upper decks.

Whenever an air attack was imminent a warning siren sent us to our quarters. Running back to G Block with other internees, I was once caught out in the open. Anti-aircraft shells were exploding above us, and I stopped to pick up a gnarled piece of steel, like the peel of a silver apple, that gleamed on the pathway. I remember that it was still hot to the touch. Often the Mustangs would shed their drop tanks before making their attack, and these tail-less, bomb-shaped structures were treated with immense respect by the guards, who roped them off and waited for army engineers to inspect them.

The air attacks on Shanghai took place almost daily, and once Lunghua airfield had been neutralised the first waves of B-29 bombers appeared in the sky, immense four-engined aircraft that bombed the airfield, Shanghai dockyards and railway junctions. They passed overhead and then seemed to vanish into the clouds, and a moment later a thunderous curtain of smoke rose from the ground as sticks of bombs struck the hangars and parked planes. I can still see one Mustang trailing smoke that turned and headed east towards the sea, the pilot hoping perhaps to ditch his crippled plane near a US warship. As the Mustang crossed the Whangpoo he seemed to give up, and we saw his parachute open and a truck filled with Japanese soldiers driving past the camp to capture him.

The sight of these advanced American aircraft gave me a new focus of adolescent veneration. As the Mustangs streaked overhead, less than a hundred feet from the ground, it was clear that they belonged to a different technological order. The power of their engines (the British-designed Rolls-Royce Merlin, I later learned), their speed and silver fuselages, and the high style in which they were flown, clearly placed them in a more advanced realm than the Japanese Zeros and the Spitfires and Hurricanes of the British Embassy newsreels. The American aircraft had sprung from the advertisement pages of *Life* and *Collier's*, they embodied the same consumer ethos as the streamlined Cadillacs and Lincoln Zephyrs, the refrigerators and radios. In a way the Mustangs and Lightnings were themselves advertisements, 400-mile-an-hour commercials that advertised the American dream and American power.

I noticed that the American seamen in E Block took for granted the superiority of the advanced aircraft flying over their heads. Despite the catastrophe that befell the battleships *Repulse* and *Prince of Wales*, the British internees still spoke with a certain dogged pride of their country's military equipment. But the American seamen I visited said nothing and never made a boastful claim.

All this led me to switch my boyhood admiration to a new set of heroes. However brave the Japanese soldiers and pilots, they belonged to the past. America, I knew, was a future that had already arrived. I spent every spare moment watching the sky.

9

The Railway Station (1945)

One day in early August we woke to find that the Japanese guards had gone. We assembled for the morning roll-call, standing in the corridor outside our rooms, but the guards failed to appear. We wandered away, listening to the empty sky. One or two reconnaissance planes drifted high overhead, but for the first time everything was silent. Had the war ended? Rumours and counter-rumours swept the camp, but Lunghua was sealed off from the world, surrounded by the deserted villages and drained paddy fields.

Demoralised by the unending air offensive and the sinking of most of their shipping by American submarines near the Yangtze estuary, and by the loss of Iwo Jima and Okinawa, the Japanese military responsible for Lunghua Camp had finally abandoned this malaria-ridden group of foreign internees. The food supply had been intermittent for months, and I spent hours on the observation roof of F Block, hoping for any sign of the Red Cross truck that would bring the next day's rations.

The perimeter fence ran within a dozen yards of G Block, and a few of the internees began to step through the barbed wire. They stood in the deep grass, inhaling the air outside the camp, as if testing a different atmosphere. I followed them and, rather than stay near the fence, I decided to walk to a burial mound some two hundred yards away. I climbed onto the lowest tier of rotting coffins, turned and looked back at the camp, a view I had never seen before. It seemed almost uncanny to be no longer part of the camp but staring at it from a distance. Everything about its perspectives seemed strange and unreal, though it had been my home for two and a half years. I jumped down from the burial mound, then ran back through the deep grass to the fence and climbed through the wire, relieved to be back in the camp and the only security I knew.

Emboldened by the absence of the Japanese guards, a number of British internees decided to walk to Shanghai. I was tempted to join them, but fortunately decided not to. Within hours they were brought back to the camp, lying badly beaten on the floor of a Japanese truck, part of a motorised unit of military police that immediately re-established control over Lunghua. I assume that at this time the first atomic bomb had been dropped on Hiroshima, but the Japanese had not yet decided to surrender. The Japanese generals in China were still prepared to fight on to the end, aware that most of Japan's principal cities and industrial areas had been reduced to ash by the American bombing campaign.

The Japanese soldiers stepped down from their trucks, and seized a number of internees and held them for interrogation in the first-floor offices of the commandant and his staff in F Block. Realising what might happen to their husbands, a group of wives attacked the Japanese as they crossed the assembly ground outside D Block, then formed up below the balcony of the commandant's offices, jeering and screaming at the Japanese officers as they stared down impassively at the raging women. The spit from their mouths formed necklaces on their breasts as they swore and shook their fists at the Japanese.

Eventually the men were released, but still no one knew if the war had ended. A few days later we heard of Hirohito's broadcast, calling on Japanese forces everywhere to lay down their arms, but we were all unsure whether they would obey him, even when the Japanese guards finally drove away from Lunghua and left us to ourselves. The bombing raids had ceased, but Japanese military units still occupied Shanghai and the surrounding countryside.

It was several weeks before American forces arrived in strength to take control of Shanghai. August 1945 formed a strange interregnum when we were never wholly certain that the war had ended, a sensation that stayed with me for months and even years. To this day as I doze in an armchair I feel the same brief moment of uncertainty.

*   *   *

I stayed in the camp, waiting until I was sure that the Japanese had surrendered. All sense of community spirit had left Lunghua, and nothing seemed to matter any more. The school had closed, and children played their skipping games while their mothers abandoned the family washing on the lines behind G Block. But the water from the Bubbling Well station was cold, and the Red Cross sent a daily tanker filled with drinking water to the camp, along with enough rations to keep us going. Clearly, though, the camp's reason for existence had passed. I wandered around the ruined buildings with Cyril Goldbert, listening to him describe the Shakespeare roles he would soon be playing, 'his' Hamlet, Othello and Macbeth, aware that none of us in Lunghua had any role at all.

Then, in the last days of August, I was on the roof of F Block when a B-29 flew towards the camp at a height of about 800 feet. Its bomb doors were open, and for a few seconds I assumed that we were about to be attacked. A line of canisters fell from the bomb bays, parachutes flared and the first American relief supplies floated towards us. A stampede followed, as everyone helped to drag the canisters back to their blocks. Each one was a cargo of treasure, but a sensible rationing system saw that every family received its fair share. There were tins of Spam and Klim, cartons of Lucky Strike cigarettes, cans of jam and huge bars of chocolate. I remember vividly our first meal on our little card table, and the extraordinary taste of animal fat, sugar, jam and chocolate. The vast lazy planes that floated overhead were emissaries from another world. The camp came alive again, as the internees found a new purpose in their lives. Everyone hoarded and guarded their new supplies, listening out for the sound of American engines, quick to point out the smallest unfairness.

Tired of all this, and revived by the Spam and chocolate, I decided to walk to Shanghai. I had spent years staring at the apartment houses of the French Concession, and I was eager to see Amherst Avenue again. Without telling my parents, I set off for the fence behind the old shower blocks. Confident that I could walk the five miles to the western suburbs of Shanghai, I stepped through the wire.

The camp fell behind me more quickly than I expected. Around me was a silent terrain of abandoned paddy fields and burial mounds, derelict canals and bridges, ghost villages that had been deserted for years. I skirted the perimeter of the airfield, where I could see Japanese soldiers patrolling the burnt-out planes and hangars, and decided not to test whether they agreed that the war was over. I passed the wrecks of canal boats and trucks caught in the air attacks, and the bodies of Chinese puppet soldiers.

After an hour I reached the Hangchow–Shanghai railway line, which circled the western perimeter of Shanghai. No trains were running, and I decided to walk along the embankment. Half a mile in front of me was a small wayside station, no more than a concrete platform and a pair of telegraph poles. As I approached I could hear an odd sing-song sound, and saw that a group of Japanese soldiers was waiting on the platform. They were fully armed, and sat on their ammunition boxes, picking their teeth while one of them tormented a young Chinese man in black trousers and a white shirt. The Japanese soldier had cut down lengths of telephone wire and had tied the Chinese to a telegraph pole, and was now slowly strangling him as the Chinese sang out in a sing-song voice. I thought of leaving the embankment and walking across the nearby field, but then decided it would be best to walk straight up to the soldiers and treat the grim event taking place as if it were a private matter that did not involve me.

I drew level with the platform and was about to walk past it when the soldier with the telephone wire raised a hand and beckoned me towards him. He had seen the transparent celluloid belt that held up my frayed cotton shorts. It had been given to me by one of the American sailors, and was a prized novelty that no Japanese was likely to have seen. I unbuckled the belt and handed it to him, then waited as he flexed the colourless plastic and stared at me through it, laughing admiringly. Behind him the young Chinese was slowly suffocating to death, his urine spreading across the platform.

I waited in the sun, listening to the sing-song voice as it

grew weaker. The Chinese was not the first person I had seen the Japanese kill. But a state of war had existed since 1937, and now peace was supposed to have come to the mouth of the Yangtze. At the same time I was old enough to know that this lost Japanese platoon was beyond the point where life and death meant anything at all. They were aware that their own lives would shortly end, and that they were free to do anything they wanted, and inflict any pain. Peace, I realised, was more threatening because the rules that sustained war, however evil, were suspended. The empty paddy fields and derelict villages confirmed that nothing mattered.

Ten minutes later, the Chinese was silent and I was able to walk away. The Japanese soldier never told me to go, but I knew when he had lost interest in me. Whistling to himself, the plastic belt around his neck, he stepped over the trussed body of the Chinese and rejoined his companions, waiting for the train that would never come.

I was badly shaken, but managed to steady myself by the time I reached the western suburbs of Shanghai. Perhaps the war had not really ended, or we had entered an in-between world where on one level it would continue for months or even years, merging into the next war and the war beyond that. I like to think that my teenage self kept his nerve, but I realise now that I was probably aware of nothing other than the brute fact that I was alive and this unknown Chinese was dead. In most respects, sadly, my experiences of the war were no different from those of millions of other teenage boys in enemy-occupied Europe and the Far East. A vast cruelty lay over the world, and was all we knew.

At last I reached the western suburbs of Shanghai, and set off for the Kendall-Ward house. I needed to see them again, after a lapse of nearly three years. I knew the boys would have grown, and the Airedales would be older, but Mrs Kendall-Ward would be the same, a little thinner but as welcoming as ever. I could already hear her chatting in Chinese to her tribe of amahs, as the dogs bounded around her.

The gates were ajar, and I walked up the drive past the untended garden, listening for any sounds of the family. I reached for the doorbell, and looked through the open door at the sky. It took me several moments to realise what had happened. The house was a shell. Everything had been looted and stripped away, every door frame, joist and floor-board, every roof beam and tile, every electric cable and water pipe. Nothing remained except the raw brickwork. The unguarded house had become, in effect, a free carpentry store and hardware shop, where local Chinese had helped themselves to whatever electrical switch or faucet they needed. I remember feeling a profound sense of loss, as if a large part of the happiness I had known in pre-war Shanghai had been erased for ever. It was a grave mistake to rely on one's memories, which were as much a stage set as the gutted house whose doorbell I was trying to ring.

After resting on the doorstep, I walked down Amherst Avenue to the Ballard house at 31, expecting to find it similarly stripped. I climbed the steps, and heard the doorbell ring. A young puppet soldier, a Chinese youth not much older than I was, opened the door and tried to bar my way with his rifle. I pushed past him, saying: 'This is my house.'

A Chinese puppet general had occupied the house, but had fled the scene, no doubt in a complete panic after the Japanese surrender. The house was untouched, every piece of furniture and kitchen equipment in place. I walked around the airless rooms, watching the sunlight play on the swirls of dust that followed me. I climbed the stairs to my bedroom, and lay on the bed, counting the screw-hooks from which I had hung my model aircraft. The house seemed strange, and I felt that it should have changed, like everything else in Shanghai. It was almost as if the war had never happened.

10

War's End (1945)

Shanghai soon opened all its doors and turned on all its lights, greeting its new American visitors in its time-honoured way, with thousands of bars, prostitutes and gambling dens. An American cruiser moored off the Bund, and American aircraft landed at Lunghua airfield, but the transfer of power took several weeks to become effective. Disbanded puppet troops and aimless militia units still roamed the outskirts of the city, and most of the Lunghua internees remained for the next month within the comparative safety of the camp.

I went back to Shanghai several times, walking or cadging lifts from Red Cross drivers, or riding on top of the tanker that brought fresh water to the camp. One afternoon in Shanghai I set off on the five-mile walk back to Lunghua, following the road that led to the airfield. An hour later a Japanese army truck passed me. I ran after the wheezing vehicle and then clambered uninvited over the tailboard.

Half a dozen armed Japanese soldiers watched me as I sat down next to them, and one took the water bottle from my hand. He tasted the water with a grimace, perhaps hoping for something stronger, and passed it back to me. When I jumped down at the next crossroads and set off across the paddy fields for Lunghua one of them might easily have shot me, for they must have had only the faintest idea of Hirohito's surrender broadcast. But they may have realised that in some way I was on their side.

The Ballard family left Lunghua at the beginning of September, and returned to their house in Amherst Avenue. A staff of servants signed on, though I'm not sure if they included any of those dismissed when we went to Lunghua. Our former chauffeur returned, driving a Chrysler that my father had bought from one of his Chinese business contacts. Huge quantities of gifts arrived daily at our house, straw panniers filled with fresh peaches and mangoes, canned goods and bottles of pre-war Scotch whisky. I remember live chickens strutting and squawking around the hall until they were seized by the cook and taken off to the kitchen.

I at last made contact with the Kendall-Wards, who had survived the war and were now living in a rented house to the north-west of the city. I was glad to see the boys again, and Mrs Kendall-Ward greeted me warmly. But I felt slightly uneasy with them all. Miraculously, they seemed unchanged by the war, as charming and amiable as ever.

But I had changed, and I knew that childhood had passed for good.

Yet within a surprisingly short time something very close to our previous life resumed. Dozens of American warships were moored in the Whangpoo, and armed shore parties of American sailors and marines were moving around Shanghai. The German family who lived in the house across the drive were ejected, and two very likeable American intelligence officers took their place. They soon moved in their stylish Chinese girlfriends, educated and sophisticated women who brought my mother up to date with the latest fashion news. The Americans were part of the military administration of Shanghai, and would take me with them on trips around the city, visiting the stockades where Japanese soldiers and Chinese collaborators were imprisoned, in the grimmest conditions. In the evenings they would hold film shows and invite the Ballards over. We watched the Andrews Sisters singing 'Don't Fence Me In', and joined in heartily, following the bouncing ball. The Americans had unlimited supplies of magazines and comics, but I was more interested in the wartime pocket editions of Hemingway and Steinbeck, which I devoured. The shortage of paper in Lunghua meant that I had done little writing, but Hemingway's accounts of the Great War tallied with my own memories of war and the unwelcome truths it could expose.

My father arranged for me to be given a bicycle by a Chinese business friend, and I began to pedal around

Shanghai again. I often went out to Lunghua airfield, and was invited aboard the huge American transport planes lined up beside the runway. The sense of American power was overwhelming. I also made regular visits to Lunghua Camp. At least half the internees still lived there two months after the war's end, sustained by the American airdrops. These were Britons with no homes to return to, no jobs, and no source of income, waiting to be repatriated to England.

The atmosphere in Lunghua had clearly changed. When I dismounted from my new cycle at the gates I was stopped by a former D Block internee whose son had been a close camp friend. He wore a large American pistol in a holster, and affected the manner of a military policeman. He pretended not to recognise me, and refused to allow me through the gates until I had gone through a pantomime of convincing him who I was.

In G Block the families who remained had taken over the empty rooms, and the Ballard room was now a storehouse of air-dropped supplies. Ends of corridors were barricaded off, and visitors were no longer welcome. During one visit a B-29 dropping relief supplies misjudged the target, and the coloured parachutes sailed down into the untended paddy fields half a mile from the camp. Within a minute a posse of internees, some armed with rifles, left the camp and raced towards the drifting parachutes. I followed at a distance, and saw the violent confrontation between the internees and a group of destitute peasants dragging a canister towards their village. Needless to say, it never occurred to the internees that China had fought on the same side against the Japanese, and that their desperate citizens were even more deserving of relief.

Later, in England, I heard that many of the Lunghua internees were still living in the camp six months after the war's end, defending their caches of Spam, Klim and cartons of Lucky Strike cigarettes.

In many ways I missed the camp, and the hundreds of acquaintances I had made of all ages. I missed the chess games, and the American sailors, and the teenage girls teaching each other how to flirt. I felt more at home there than I did at 31 Amherst Avenue. Prison, which so confines the adults, offers unlimited scope to the imagination of a teenage boy. The moment I stepped out of bed in the morning, as my mother slept in her tattered mosquito net and my father tried to brew a little tea for her, a hundred possibilities waited for me.

At least Shanghai was coming alive again, as thousands of American servicemen filled the bars and nightclubs and careered around the streets in their jeeps and trucks. Pedicabs had appeared, large two-seater tricycles, pedalled by former rickshaw coolies, usually filled by two Americans and their Russian and Chinese girlfriends. Led by my father, China Printing began to produce the cotton goods that the Far East needed so desperately. Bizarrely, armed Japanese sentries, on the orders of the Americans, still guarded key locations in Shanghai, just as the French regaining control of Indo-China used Japanese military units in their battles against the Viet Minh forces, the forerunners of the Viet Cong.

I knew that I would be going to England with my mother and sister on one of the troopships that were repatriating the British internees, and also that I would be going to school in England, but it never occurred to me that I would make a final break with Shanghai and not return for forty-five years. No one had the faintest inkling that the lights of Shanghai would be switched off for decades when the Communists led by Mao Tse-tung took control. Every Westerner in the city took it for granted that the puritan self-discipline of the Chinese Communists would last just as long as it took them to climb from their tanks and stroll into the bars and brothels of downtown Shanghai.

At the end of 1945 my mother, my sister Margaret and I boarded the SS *Arrawa*, and set sail on the voyage to England. The *Arrawa* was a former refrigerated cargo vessel used as a troopship during the war, and the decks and holds were lined with miles of refrigeration piping. Some thousand British internees came aboard, and there was a huge send-off at the pier in Hongkew. Friends and relatives who were staying behind lined the pier and waved as the ship moved out into the Whangpoo, surrounded by scores of American landing craft sounding their sirens. My mother and sister were at the rail, somewhere amidships, but I moved to the stern to be on my own. At the last minute my father turned from my mother and waved to me, and for some reason I have never understood I decided not to wave back. I assume he thought I had lost sight of him, but I have always regretted not waving to him. Apart from a visit he made to England in 1947, when we drove all over Europe, I did not see him again until 1950. By then we had grown apart, and he played no role in the many decisions I had made about my future career.

The voyage was in some ways like a seaboard version of Lunghua in its earliest days, everyone in beachwear as we headed for Singapore and the equator. We docked briefly at Rangoon, and the captain told us that a party of thirty British commandos were joining us. He warned mothers of teenage daughters to be on their guard. These violent and ruthless men had been fighting the Japanese, and would pose a danger to any young English women they came across.

I and my friends were all agog at the prospect and keenly awaited developments. The commandos came aboard, heavily armed young men with sunburnt English faces. They stowed their weapons in the armoury, and then made straight for the passenger saloon on the upper deck, where they spent the rest of the voyage. Every morning when they arrived they would each buy ten bottles of beer from the bar and carry them to their tables, so that the entire surface was filled with beer bottles. Sitting back in the leather arm-chairs, they passed the rest of the day drinking, rarely saying anything to each other and taking no interest in the teenage English girls who came in to smile at them.

This deeply impressed me, and still does. I and my friends questioned them about the bitter battles they had fought with Japanese soldiers, many of them starving and suicidal, but the commandos were reluctant to talk. Now and then they would praise a dead comrade who had died beside them as they fought off the Japanese bayonet charges. At Southampton, when we moored, they snapped back into life, reclaimed their weapons and marched off smartly without a backward glance. That also impressed me. Some of them were only two or three years older than I was. They had seen death run towards them armed with a bayonet and a grenade, and had fought him to a standstill.

PART II

11

Take it on the Chin (1946)

Winter numbed, England froze.

The *Arrawa* docked at Southampton, under a cold sky so grey and low that I could hardly believe this was the England I had read and heard about. Small, putty-faced people moved around, shabbily dressed and with a haunted air. Looking down from the rail, I noticed that the streets near the docks were lined with what seemed to be black perambulators, some kind of mobile coal scuttle, I assumed, used for bunkering ships. Later I learned that these were British cars (all made pre-war), a species I had never seen before.

We travelled to London, and then went on to West Bromwich, where I met my grandparents. Our mutual suspicion was probably instant. After a month or so I entered The Leys School in Cambridge as a boarder, and my mother rented a house at Newton Ferrers, about ten miles from Plymouth, near Shanghai friends. I joined her during the holidays, but in 1947 she and my sister returned to Shanghai with my father, and for the next year or so I spent the holidays with my grandparents in West Bromwich, the lowest point in my life that I had by then explored, several miles at least below the sea level of mental health. I hope that I survived, though I have never been completely sure. My mother returned to England with my sister in 1949, and rented a house in the Aldwick Bay estate, to the west of Bognor. After my father's escape from China, when I was at King's College, Cambridge, they moved to Manchester. When he left the Calico Printers Association they bought a house in Claygate, near Esher, and in the early 1960s retired to the New Forest.

My first impressions of England remained vividly in my mind for years. They may seem unnecessarily hostile, but they were no different from the impressions that England made on countless American GIs and the Canadian and American students I met at Cambridge. Even allowing for a long and exhausting war, England seemed derelict, dark and half-ruined. The Southampton that greeted me as I carried my suitcase down the gangway had been heavily bombed during the war, and consisted largely of rubble, with few signs of human settlement. Large sections of London and the Midlands were vast bomb sites, and most of the buildings still standing were ruined and desolate. London and greater Birmingham, like the other main cities, had been built in the 19th century, and everything seemed to be crumbling and shabby, unpainted for years, and in many ways resembled a huge demolition site. Few buildings dated from the 1930s, though I never visited the vast London suburbs that largely survived the war intact. A steady drizzle fell for most of the time, and the sky was slate-grey with soot lifting over the streets from tens of thousands of chimneys. Everything was dirty, and the interiors of railway carriages and buses were black with grime.

Looking at the English people around me, it was impossible to believe that they had won the war. They behaved like a defeated population. I wrote in *The Kindness of Women* that the English talked as if they had won the war, but acted as if they had lost it. They were clearly exhausted by the war, and expected little of the future. Everything was rationed – food, clothing, petrol – or simply unobtainable. People moved in a herd-like way, queueing for everything. Ration books and clothing coupons were all-important, endlessly counted and fussed over, even though there was almost nothing in the shops to buy. Tracking down a few light bulbs could take all day. Everything was poorly designed – my grandparents' three-storey house was heated by one or two single-bar electric fires and an open coal fire. Most of the house was icy, and we slept under huge eiderdowns like marooned Arctic travellers in their survival gear, a frozen air numbing our faces, the plumes of our breath visible in the darkness.

More importantly, hope itself was rationed, and people's spirits were bent low. The only hope came from Hollywood films, and long queues, often four abreast, formed outside the immense Odeons and Gaumonts that had survived the bombing. The people waiting in the rain for their hour or two of American glamour were docile and resigned. The impression given by the newsreels we had seen in Shanghai, of confident crowds celebrating VE and VJ Days, wasn't remotely borne out by the people huddling in the drizzle outside their local cinema, the only recreation apart from the BBC radio programmes, which were dominated by maniacal English comedians (*ITMA*, totally incomprehensible) or *Workers' Playtime* (forced cheerfulness relayed from factories).

It took a long while for this mood to lift, and food rationing went on into the 1950s. But there was always the indirect rationing of simple unavailability, and the far more dangerous rationing of any kind of belief in a better life. The whole nation seemed to be deeply depressed. Audiences sat in their damp raincoats in smoke-filled cinemas as they watched newsreels that showed the immense pomp of the royal family, the aggressively cheerful crowds at a new holiday camp, and the triumph of some new air-speed or land-speed record, as if Britain led the world in technology. It is hard to imagine how conditions could have been worse if we had lost the war.

It came home to me very quickly that the England I had been brought up to believe in – A.A. Milne, *Just William*, *Chums* annuals – was a complete fantasy. The English middle class had lost its confidence. Even the relatively well-off friends of my parents – doctors, lawyers, senior managers – had a very modest standard of living, large but poorly heated homes, and a dull and very meagre diet. Few of them went abroad, and most of their pre-war privileges, such as domestic servants and a comfortable lifestyle awarded to them by right, were now under threat.

For the first time, I was meeting large numbers of working-class people, with a range of regional accents that took a trained ear to decode. Travelling around the Birmingham area, I was amazed at how bleakly they lived, how poorly paid they were, poorly educated, housed and fed. To me they were a vast exploited workforce, not much better off than the industrial workers in Shanghai. I think it was clear to me from the start that the English class system, which I was meeting for the first time, was an instrument of political control, and not a picturesque social relic. Middle-class people in the late 1940s and 1950s saw the working class as almost another species, and fenced themselves off behind a complex system of social codes.

Most of these I had to learn now for the first time – show respect to one's elders, never be too keen, take it on the chin, be decent to the junior ranks, defer to tradition, stand up for the national anthem, offer leadership, be modest and so on, all calculated to create a sense of overpowering deference, and certainly not qualities that had made Shanghai great or, for that matter, won the Battle of Britain. Everything about English middle-class life revolved around codes of behaviour that unconsciously cultivated second-rateness and low expectations.

With its ancestor worship and standing to attention for 'God Save the King', England needed to be freed from itself and from the delusions that people in all walks of life clung to about Britain's place in the world. Most of the British adults I met genuinely thought that we had won the war singlehandedly, with a little help, often more of a hindrance, from the Americans and Russians. In fact we had suffered enormous losses, exhausted and impoverished ourselves, and had little more to look forward to than our nostalgia.

Should we have gone to war in 1939, given how ill-prepared we were, and how little we did to help Poland, to whose aid Neville Chamberlain had committed us when he declared war on Germany? Despite all our efforts, the loss of a great many brave lives and the destruction of our cities, Poland was rapidly overrun by the Germans and became the greatest slaughterhouse in history. Should Britain and France have waited a few years, until the Russians had broken the back of German military power? And, most important from my point of view, would the Japanese have attacked Pearl Harbor if they had known that they faced not only the Americans but the French, British and Dutch armies, navies and air forces? The sight of the three colonial powers defeated or neutralised by the Germans must have tipped the balance in Japanese calculations.

In short, did the English pay a fearful price for the system of self-delusions that underpinned almost everything in their lives? The question seemed to leap from the shabby streets and bomb sites when I first came to England, and played a large role in the difficulty I had settling down here. It fed into my troubled sense of who I was, and encouraged me to think of myself as a lifelong outsider and maverick. It probably steered me towards becoming a writer devoted to predicting and, if possible, provoking change. Change, I felt, was what England desperately needed, and I still feel it.

The Leys School, 1946–49

Life at an English boarding school was part of the continuum of strangeness that made up my adolescence. I once said that The Leys reminded me of Lunghua Camp, though the food was worse. In fact, by the standards prevalent among English public schools, The Leys was liberal and progressive. It had been founded in 1875 by rich Nonconformists from the north of England, who wanted the ethos and discipline of a public school without the mummery and flummery of the Church of England. Most of the founders were industrialists, and were strong supporters of science. The large science block at The Leys was remarkably well-equipped, with superb physics, chemistry and biology labs, so much so that I rather looked down on the tired and broken equipment I later found in the University science laboratories. The school had a large swimming pool, the only indoor pool in Cambridge when I was there, regularly used for University events. There was no fagging, and though there was chapel twice a day, many of the Sunday sermons were given by lay preachers, often well-known scientists. The Methodist message was never blatant.

Another advantage was that the school was in Cambridge. Most public schools existed in an isolated world of their own, but The Leys was within walking distance of the centre of Cambridge. This was important to me, and meant that I was able to visit friends from the classes above mine who had entered the University a year ahead of me. It gave me an early taste of college life, and access to excellent bookshops, specialist journals and student magazines I would never have seen otherwise.

Above all, there was the Arts Cinema, where I saw virtually the entire repertory of French, Italian, Swedish and German films screened in England after the war. I remember Carné's *Les Enfants du Paradis*, a wonderful romp of wartime collaborators led by Arletty; Clouzot's *Le Corbeau* and *Manon* (with the divine child-woman Cécile Aubry, apparently no older than I was and impossible to get out of my 17-year-old head); Cocteau's *Orphée*, with another 'divine', María Casares, incarnating Death: I was more than ready to die as I recuperated in the Copper Kettle, a coffee shop on King's Parade, before going back to cottage pie and treacle pudding in the school dining hall; Wolfgang Staudte's *The Murderers are Among Us*, the first revisionist German film, powerful but hollow.

I also liked American films, especially the B-movies that formed the lower part of a double bill. This was the heyday of film noir, and I must have sneaked away on our free afternoons to see everything that the Hollywood studios could produce. I devoured *Double Indemnity* (Barbara Stanwyck reminded me in some ways of my mother and her bridge-playing friends, desperate women trying to break out of their housewifely roles) and Robert Mitchum in *Out of the Past*, but my favourite films of all were the ultra-low-budget crime and gangster movies. These were often far more interesting than the star vehicle topping the bill. Out of the simplest materials – two cars, a cheap motel, a gun and a tired brunette – they conjured up a hard and unsentimental image of the primeval city, a psychological space that existed first and foremost in the characters' minds.

Writing my short stories in idle moments during evening prep, I knew that the post-war film offered a serious challenge to any aspirant writer. The novel thrived on static societies, which the novelist could examine like an entomologist labelling a tray of butterflies. But too much had happened to me, and to the boys sitting at the desks around me, in the wartime years. Continuous upheavals had unsettled family life: fathers were away in the Middle East or in the Pacific, mothers had taken on jobs and responsibilities that had redefined who they felt they were. People had memories of bombing raids and beachheads, endless hours of queueing and waiting in provincial railway stations that were impossible to convey to anyone not actually there. I never talked about my life in Shanghai or internment in Lunghua even to my closest friends. Too much had happened for even a race of novelists to digest. But I persisted with my short sketches, gnawing away at the inner bone.

Despite its modern ways, The Leys was the model for the very old-fashioned public school shown in the film *Goodbye, Mr Chips*, based on a novel by an Old Leysian, the bestselling writer James Hilton (author also of the Shangri-La novel, *Lost Horizon*). Mr Chips was modelled on a master named Balgarnie, a familiar figure around the school during my years there. When Hollywood made its version of the novel, with Robert Donat, they chose a deeply self-enclosed, ivy-clad Victorian institution far removed in spirit from The Leys, all Gothic spires and hallowed cloisters.

In fact, the masters at The Leys were remarkably open-minded. They lived in Cambridge, many had served in the war, and none of them would have wanted to bring a sentimental tear to the eyes of the boys they taught. The English master, who had the closest access to the turmoil inside my head, never chided me for the strange notions I set out in my essays, which were virtually short stories, and encouraged me to read as widely as I could.

As I entered the Science VIth at 16 I was spending more and more of my time in the school library. The careers master assumed that I would go on to Cambridge University, but I was still not sure what subject I would study. My parents were in Shanghai, and I was thrown onto myself. My grandparents were in many ways as remote from me as the Chinese servants at 31 Amherst Avenue. Any kind of discussion was impossible. They were obsessed with the iniquity of the post-war Labour government, which they genuinely believed to have carried out a military putsch to seize control of the country, using the postal votes of millions of overseas servicemen. If I made the mildest comment in praise of the Prime Minister, Clement Attlee, my grandfather would stare silently at me, his face turning bright pink and then purple. Yet all around him was the desperate poverty of the Black Country, with some of the most ill-housed and poorly educated people in western Europe, still giving their lives after the war to maintain an empire that had never been of the least benefit to them. My grandfather's attitude was common, and based less on feelings of social class than on a visceral resistance to change. Change was the enemy of everything he believed in.

I spent the long months of school holiday with them reading relentlessly, sketching out 'experimental' short stories, which usually proved the experiment had failed, and going to the cinemas in Birmingham. I liked to go in the afternoons, when the vast auditoriums were almost empty, and sit in the front row of the circle, the closest possible communion with the world of the Hollywood screen. I avoided English films, apart from a select few – *A Matter of Life and Death*, a posthumous fantasy in which a 'dead' pilot walks ashore into an England he barely recognises, a predicament with which I totally identified; *The Third Man*, a masterpiece that might just as well have been set in England (the bomb sites and black market, the air of compromise and defeat, the sports jackets and shabby drinking clubs straight out of Earls Court); and the wonderful Ealing comedies, which sent up the English class system that everyone secretly accepted, for reasons I have never understood.

The more I learned about English life, the stranger it seemed, and I was unsure how I could shape my life to avoid it. The contemporary novelists I read offered little help. I enjoyed Evelyn Waugh and Graham Greene, Aldous Huxley and George Orwell, but most English novelists were far too 'English'. To save myself from the suffocations of English life, I seized on American and European writers, the whole canon of classic modernism – Hemingway, Dos Passos, Kafka, Camus, Joyce and Dostoevsky. It was probably a complete waste of time. I read far too much, far too early, long before I had any experience of adult life: the worlds of work, marriage and parenthood. I was focusing on the strong mood of alienation that dominated these writers, and on little else. In many ways I was rather lost, trying to find my way through a dark and very grim funfair where none of the lights would come on.

Then, at the age of 16, I discovered Freud and the surrealists, a stick of bombs that fell in front of me and destroyed all the bridges that I was hesitating to cross.

Freud's works, like Jung's, were easy to come across in the late 1940s, but reproductions of surrealist paintings were extremely difficult to find. Many of the first paintings I saw by Chirico, Ernst and Dalí were in books about abnormal psychology, or in guides to modern philosophy, both very popular in the years after Belsen and Hiroshima. Freud was still something of an academic joke; the admissions tutor at King's assumed that I was being ironic when I mentioned my admiration of Freud. The surrealists were still decades away from achieving any kind of critical respectability, and even serious newspapers treated them as a rather tired joke.

Needless to say, this rejection only recommended Freud and the surrealists to me. I felt strongly, and still do, that psychoanalysis and surrealism were a key to the truth about existence and the human personality, and also a key to myself. My head was filled with half-digested fragments of Kafka and Joyce, the Paris existentialists and Italian neo-realist films such as *Rome, Open City*, the high tide of heroic modernism, played out against the background of the Nazi death camps and the growing threat of nuclear war.

All this pressed around me, but I was stuck in a deeply provincial outpost, England in the late 1940s. Few of the painters, philosophers, writers and film-makers I admired were English, but at the same time I could see that I myself was becoming more and more English, if only to get along more comfortably with everyone I met. By 1948 I knew that the Communists under Mao Tse-tung would soon take over the whole of China and that I would never go back to Shanghai. Lunghua Camp and the International Settlement would be swept away. England was my home for the indefinite future, and the locks had been changed.

But surrealism and psychoanalysis offered an escape route, a secret corridor into a more real and more meaningful world, where shifting psychological roles are more important than the 'character' so admired by English schoolmasters and literary critics, and where the deep revolutions of the psyche matter more than the social dramas of everyday life, as trivial as a tempest in a tea cosy.

Freud's serene and masterful tone, his calm assumption that psychoanalysis could reveal the complete truth about modern man and his discontents, appealed to me powerfully, especially in the absence of my own father. At the same time, the surrealists' rejection of reason and rationality, their faith in the power of the imagination to remake the world, resonated strongly with my efforts as a novice writer. I wrote short stories and fragments of incomprehensible novels which made complete sense if deemed to be surrealist. Ever since childhood I had a flair for drawing, and in the art department at The Leys I made plaster casts of the faces of friends (I called them 'death' masks after those of Shelley, Blake, Napoleon and other heroes). I nearly suffocated one classmate when the plaster failed to set and I physically restrained him from clawing away the oozing carapace. To my lifelong regret, however, I lacked the skill and facility to become a painter, whereas my head was filled with short stories and I had the beginnings of a knack for expressing them.

Despite my efforts to fit in, I think I was a bit of a misfit at school, an over-aggressive tennis player who would throw a game so that I could slip away to see the latest French film at the Arts Cinema. I was introverted but physically strong, and knew from my wartime experience that most people will back away if faced with a determined threat. One of my classmates called me an 'intellectual thug', not entirely a compliment, and my years in Lunghua had probably given me a tendency to watch other boys' plates in the dining hall. I was also prone to backing up an argument about existentialism with a raised fist.

I had a few close friends, an Anglo-Indian boy who went up to Trinity a year ahead of me to study medicine, and an American exchange student. There was also a boy called Frank who was an Auschwitz survivor and had his number prominently tattooed on his arm. He was adopted after the war by an émigré Cambridge physicist and his wife, and attended The Leys as a day boy. To begin with he spoke no English, but he was well-liked. I was drawn to all of them because they were foreigners, but when my parents returned from Shanghai on a visit, my mother stepping from their new Buick, dressed in the latest New York fashions, I thought rather critically of how un-English they seemed. I knew, as I thought this, that it marked how English I was becoming, despite all my efforts. The camouflage always imitates the target.

In the Upper VIth I passed the King's College entrance examination and met the admissions tutor. I had applied to read psychology, but at the time psychology was not an independent faculty at Cambridge, and he told me that I would have to read philosophy, which contained a small element of psychology within it. 'What do you want to do when you graduate?' he asked me. When I said that I was really interested in psychiatry, he told me that I would need a medical degree. I was interested in medicine, which seemed to abut abnormal psychology and surrealism, so I agreed there and then, perhaps not the wisest decision in the long term. My parents, naturally, were delighted. In October 1949 I moved half a mile down Trumpington Street to King's, and began my study of anatomy, physiology and pathology.

As I left The Leys for the last time, entering the world as an adult, I felt more confident about the future than I had at any time since arriving in England. In the last two years at school I had read a great deal, endlessly experimented with my short stories, which were becoming steadily more unreadable, and through my study of biology had even found a strain of scientific mysticism in my imagination. I was happy with the prospect of becoming a psychiatrist, and knew that I already had my first patient – myself. I was well aware that my reasons for studying medicine were strongly influenced by my memories of wartime Shanghai, and by the horrors of the European war exposed at the Nuremberg trials. The dead Chinese I had seen as a boy still lay in their ditches within my mind, an ugly mystery that needed to be solved.

The faith in reason and rationality that dominated post-war thinking struck me as hopelessly idealistic, like the belief that the German people had been led astray by Hitler and the Nazis. I was sure that the countless atrocities in eastern Europe had taken place because the Germans involved had enjoyed the act of mass murder, just as the Japanese had enjoyed tormenting the Chinese. Reason and rationality failed to explain human behaviour. Human beings were often irrational and dangerous, and the business of psychiatry was as much with the sane as the insane.

My last act at The Leys, in the week before I left, took place in the basement kitchen in North B house, when I skinned and then boiled a rabbit. I was determined to expose the skeleton, wire it together and use it as a combined mascot and table ornament. I filled the entire building with steam and a disagreeably potent stench. The housemaster came down to stop me, but backed off when he saw that I was on an intense mission of my own. Why the rabbit skeleton was so important I can't remember.

*   *   *

Shanghai was still very close to me, and the American airbases that surrounded Cambridge were a constant reminder, as were the American airmen who visited the pubs and cinemas with their English girlfriends. I was strongly drawn to flight, and could still see the B-29s sailing slowly over Lunghua, releasing their coloured parachutes like toys thrown to desperate children. I once climbed through the fence around a British airfield and crept into one of the parking bays protected by an earth embankment. Security was lax, and none of the service crews was around. There was a four-engined bomber with a tricycle landing gear – probably a Liberator – and I swung myself through the open ventral hatchway, and sat surrounded by the clutter of equipment inside the cockpit.

Today I would have been arrested, held in a child remand centre, examined by psychologists, sent to a juvenile court, and generally made to feel like a dysfunctional and even dangerous member of society. In fact, I had touched nothing and damaged nothing, and merely gazed through a small window into a dream. I might think that England was deeply repressed and ready to be laid on the analyst's couch, but I was well aware of my own flaws. I liked to think I was rootless, but I was probably as English as anyone could be, and being rootless was anyway a huge handicap. I was drawing a curtain over my past life, accepting that I would never go back to Shanghai and would have to make a new life in England, with all that this entailed.

12

Cambridge Blues (1949)

Unlike most undergraduates – never 'students', one of count-less minor anachronisms – I knew Cambridge well when I first went up to King's. I knew the coffee shops and book-shops, I had punted on the Cam, I knew several of the colleges well, especially Trinity, I had been to the tea dances at the Dorothy, the Arts Cinema and the film society, where I had seen all the pre-war classics such as *The Seashell and the Clergyman*, and Dalí's *Un Chien Andalou* and *L'Âge d'Or*.

This had advantages and drawbacks. There was never any chance that I would be 'smitten' by the visual impact of the colleges, the Gothic presence of King's chapel, the beauty of the Backs. I went on having my hair cut at the same barbers, I bought my shoes at the same shoe shops. Had I seen Cambridge for the first time in 1949, I might have taken more from it. In a sense I was ready to leave as soon as I arrived, not the best arrangement.

On the other hand, I could concentrate on the important aspects of Cambridge – the medical and science faculties –

and ignore anything connected with 'heritage' Cambridge, which has mesmerised generations of parents, who have sacrificed so much energy and ambition into getting their children between those sacred Gothic walls. This has long been one of the most wasteful forms of English snobbery. I firmly believe that Oxford and Cambridge should be graduate universities only, at one stroke killing off this absurd status race, and at the same time benefiting all other universities.

In reality there are two Cambridges, the faculties on the one hand – history, physics, archaeology and so on – where research, lectures and laboratory work take place, and the colleges, which are residential clubs that provide poor food, a small amount of often poor teaching and the bulk of the myths about the Cambridge lifestyle. I was very happy with the first, and bored stiff by the latter.

I spent my two years studying anatomy, physiology and pathology. The tuition I received was superb, the lectures lucid and intelligent, and the anatomy demonstrators who regularly tested us were all qualified physicians specialising in surgery. Anatomy involved the extended dissection of the five parts into which the human body was divided. Physiology and pathology largely consisted of examining slides through the microscope, but anatomy was a process entirely initiated by the student, and demanded hours of patient application. The dissecting room was the gravitational centre of all medical study. If nothing else was going on we would go to the DR, put on our white coats, take our particular body part – the leg, arm or head-and-neck we were dissecting, and start work alongside our Cunningham dissection manuals (never Gray's), whose pages would soon be stained with human fat.

Before our first visit to the DR we were welcomed by Professor Harris, the head of the anatomy school. He was an inspirational lecturer, the child of a modest Welsh family too poor to send their children to university. Harris and his brother were both determined to become doctors, so the younger brother worked for six years to support the older and pay his medical school fees until he qualified. He in turn supported his younger brother for a further six years until both had gained their degrees. In his wide-ranging lectures Harris made clear his belief in the noble calling of medicine, with anatomy at its heart, and I never for a moment doubted him.

At the end of his opening lecture Harris warned that a small number of us would be unable to cope with the sight of the cadavers waiting for dissection on the glass-topped tables. Walking into that strange, low-ceilinged chamber, halfway between a nightclub and an abattoir, was an unnerving experience. The cadavers, greenish-yellow with formaldehyde, lay naked on their backs, their skins covered with scars and contusions, and seemed barely human, as if they had just been taken down from a Grünewald *Crucifixion*. Several students in my group dropped out, unable to cope with the sight of their first dead bodies, but in many ways the experience of dissection was just as overwhelming for me.

Nearly sixty years later, I still think that my two years of anatomy were among the most important of my life, and helped to frame a large part of my imagination. Both before and during the war in Shanghai I had seen a great many corpses, some at very close quarters, and like everyone else I had neutralised my emotional response by telling myself: 'This is grim, but sadly part of life.' I assume that police, firemen, paramedics, doctors and nurses react in the same way. But they, at least, are absolved from any sense of guilt or responsibility. Even as a child in Shanghai I knew that something was wrong. Most of the corpses I saw, even (indirectly) the famine and disease victims, had been killed by someone else, and childishly I felt that I was partly responsible.

Now, in 1949, only a few years later, I was dissecting dead human beings, paring back the layers of skin and fat to reach the muscles below, then separating these to reveal the nerves and blood vessels. In a way I was conducting my own autopsy on all those dead Chinese I had seen lying by the roadside as I set off for school. I was carrying out a kind of emotional and even moral investigation into my own past while discovering the vast and mysterious world of the human body.

Each term we would begin work on a new cadaver, five teams of two students dissecting a body part. A team would separate its part from the cadaver, and continue the term's dissection on its own. When the DR was closed we would leave our parts in one of the large wooden cabinets – one cabinet filled with heads, another with legs, and so on. Looking at the heaped faces with their exposed teeth, it was difficult not to think of the newsreels of Belsen and Dachau that were still being shown in cinemas when fresh accounts of Nazi atrocities came to light.

In 1949 most of the cadavers in the DR were those of doctors who had willed their bodies for dissection to the next generation of medical students. This selfless act was a remarkable tribute to the spirit of these dead doctors, who knew that they would be reduced at the end of the term to a clutch of bones and gristle tagged for the incinerator. Once, searching for the senior laboratory assistant, I strayed into the preparation room beyond the DR on the last day of term, and found a large table set with a dozen metal platters, each bearing its tagged remains of the doctors who had bequeathed their bodies, a mysterious banquet in which I had taken part. I felt, and still feel, that in a sense they had transcended death, if only briefly, living on as the last breath of their identities emerged between the fingers of the students dissecting them.

Although they were identified only by number, each of the cadavers seemed to have a distinct personality – the girth and general physique, the profile bones of the face coming through the skin and reasserting themselves, the scars and blemishes, odd anomalies such as extra nipples and toes, residues of operations, tattoos, inexplicable blemishes, the story of a lifetime written into the skin, especially of the hands and face. Dissecting the face, revealing the layers of muscles and nerves that generated expressions and emotions, was a way of entering the private lives of these dead physicians and almost of bringing them back to life.

There was one female cadaver, a strong-jawed woman of late middle age, whose bald head shone brightly under the lights. Most of the male medical students gave her a wide berth. None of us had seen a naked woman of our mothers' age, alive or dead, and there was a certain authority in her face, perhaps that of a senior gynaecologist or GP. I was drawn to her, though not for the obvious sexual reasons; her breasts had subsided into the fatty tissue on her chest, and many of the students assumed she was male. But I was intrigued by the small scars on her arms, the calluses on her hands she had probably carried from childhood, and tried to reconstruct the life she had led, the long years as a medical student, her first affairs, marriage and children. One day I found her dissected head in the locker among the other heads. The exposed layers of muscles in her face were like the pages of an ancient book, or a pack of cards waiting to be reshuffled into another life.

And all the while, in a wooden box under my bed at King's, slept the bones of a small Asian farmer who had once planted rice, smoked his pipe in the evenings and watched his grandchildren grow. After his death his body had been boiled down to the white sticks that were sold on to an English medical student who had once boiled a rabbit to its bones. His skeleton, in the same pine box, has probably guided generations of Cambridge students, who have sat at their desks and explored his ribs and pelvis, feeling the bony points of his skull as if assembling the armature of a soul. Patiently, he has lived on.

My years in the dissection room were important because they taught me that though death was the end, the human imagination and the human spirit could triumph over our own dissolution. In many ways my entire fiction is the dissection of a deep pathology that I had witnessed in Shanghai and later in the post-war world, from the threat of nuclear war to the assassination of President Kennedy, from the death of my wife to the violence that underpinned the entertainment culture of the last decades of the century. Or it may be that my two years in the dissecting room were an unconscious way of keeping Shanghai alive by other means.

At all events, by the time I completed the anatomy course I had really completed my time at Cambridge. It had supplied me with a huge stock of memories, of mysterious feelings for the dead doctors who in a sense had come to my aid, and with a vast fund of anatomical metaphors that would thread through all my fiction. The hours in the dissecting room were backed up by the anatomy lectures and the time I spent reading in the anatomy library, where I became friends with an émigré Pole who was an assistant librarian, had served in the Polish Army and escaped to the West through Iraq.

By comparison, college life seemed like a quaint and overly folkloric pageant. Where the Cambridge science faculties (Rutherford and the Cavendish, Crick/Watson and DNA, Sanger and so on) were powerfully oriented towards the future, the Cambridge colleges looked back to the past. King's was dominated by its chapel and the musical events that surrounded it. The provost was a classicist, a pantomime parody of the eccentric don. In the dining hall we listened to a long Latin grace that I still know by heart, and sat on benches to eat execrable meals, wearing gowns after dusk and being overseen in the streets of Cambridge by a proctor and his bulldogs (his bowler-hatted aides). We had to be back in college by ten, or perhaps earlier. The colleges may have begun as religious foundations, but they had evolved into bizarre public schools with the boys played by adults and the masters by overgrown boys. The French and American students I knew were mystified by it all. I found it rather sad and all too typical of England at the time.

A drawback of the collegiate system is that it is difficult to make close friends in other colleges. There were no more than nine or ten medical students at King's across all three years, and I was forced to find friends who were reading other subjects. One Kingsman I knew was Simon Raven, whom I would meet in the Copper Kettle after dinner. He told me many years later that he thoroughly enjoyed his time at King's. But he was actively homosexual, and King's was an openly homosexual college, famously home to Maynard Keynes and E.M. Forster, with close connections to the painter Duncan Grant and the Bloomsbury Group. A few years earlier a number of its dons had come very near to being prosecuted for offences against the little troupe of choirboys (in miniature top hats and bum-freezer jackets) who arrived in a crocodile every day from the King's choir school. The complaining parents who threatened to go to the police were said to have been paid for their silence from the deep King's coffers.

The ethos of the college was homosexual, and a heterosexual like myself who brought in his girlfriends (mostly Addenbrooke's Hospital nurses and free-livers all) was viewed as letting the side down, as well as having made a curious choice in the first place. This was an era when most public schoolboys met no women for the first twenty years of their lives other than the school matron and their mothers, with the result that women in general remained forever in a dead perceptual zone (like vertical stripes to kittens only allowed to see horizontal stripes). I have known women married to unresponsive men they suspected of being repressed homosexuals, but most were probably victims of a special kind of English deprivation.

Otherwise, I enjoyed myself like other students, punting on the river, playing tennis, writing short stories, getting drunk with the Addenbrooke's nurses, who generously provided me with an education not even the dissecting room could match. They were interesting young women, some with remarkably rackety lives (the syringes in the bedside table drawer?) and I liked them all.

I also, with everyone else, went to a great many films. I relished hard-edged American thrillers with their expressive black and white photography and brooding atmosphere, their tales of alienation and emotional betrayal. Already I sensed that a new kind of popular culture was emerging that played on the latent psychopathy of its audiences, and in fact needed to elicit that strain of psychopathy if it was to work. The modern movement had demonstrated this from its start, in the poetry of Baudelaire and Rimbaud, and the willing engagement of the audience's own psychopathy is almost a definition of modernism as a whole. But this was strongly denied by F.R. Leavis and his notion of the novel as a moral criticism of life. I went to one of Leavis's lectures and thought how limited his world was, and remember saying to the English literature student who had taken me: 'It's more important to go to *T-Men* (a classic noir film) than to Leavis's lectures.' It sounded preposterous at the time, but less so now.

I briefly met E.M. Forster at a King's sherry party, already an old man or convincingly posing as one, and often drove in a friend's car around the US airbases. No one seemed aware that the nostalgic pageant called 'Cambridge' was made possible by the fleets of American bombers waiting in the quiet fields around the city.

At the end of my second year I knew that I had absorbed all I needed from the medical course. My interest in psychiatry had been a clear case of 'physician, heal thyself'. I never wanted to walk the wards as a trainee doctor, and friends ahead of me at their London teaching hospitals warned that years of exhausting work would postpone for at least a decade any plans to become a writer. *Varsity*, the student weekly newspaper, staged an annual short story competition, and my entry, a Hemingwayesque effort called 'The Violent Noon', won joint first prize in 1951. The judge was a senior partner at a leading London agents, A.P. Watt, who commended my story and invited me to call on him.

This was another green light, and I told my father that I wanted to give up medicine and become a writer. He was dismayed, especially as I had no idea of how to bring this about. He decided that I should study English literature, the worst possible preparation for a writer's career, which he may well have suspected. I managed to get a place at London University, at Queen Mary College, and started the degree course in October 1951.

I had written a number of short stories at Cambridge, heavily under the influence of James Joyce, and had sent a few unsuccessfully to *Horizon* and other literary magazines.

The surrealist painters were deeply inspiring, but there was no easy way to translate the visually surreal into prose, or prose that was readable. At heart I was an old-fashioned storyteller with a lively imagination, but English fantasy was too close to whimsy. This created problems that would take me a good many years to solve.

13

Screaming Popes (1951)

I enjoyed my year at Queen Mary College, glad to become a student rather than an undergraduate. I travelled on the London tube system with people who were going to work, and I could almost imagine that I was doing a job. I was one of those millions of European students who had helped to launch revolutions and had battled with police on the streets of eastern Europe, a political power bloc in their own right, something one could never imagine in the case of Oxford or Cambridge undergraduates. A student, Gavrilo Princip, had assassinated Archduke Ferdinand in Sarajevo and launched a world war. At Cambridge, an academic theme park where I was a reluctant extra, the only splash I could have made was by falling off a punt.

I liked London, and particularly the Chelsea area, with its lesbian pubs and rich friends of friends who took me to expensive nightclubs like the Milroy and Embassy in Mayfair. People lived in the present, and no one cared about property values or redecorating their flats. Everything was still very shabby and much of South Kensington, where I had a room in Onslow Gardens, was semi-derelict. People lived in dilapidated flats but bought their clothes in Bond Street. One of the English lecturers, a woman in her forties who lived nearby, owned an open-topped Allard, an impressively stylish car, which she drove all the way to the Mile End Road, a journey unthinkable today. Sometimes she gave me a lift. As we roared through the City of London she would take both hands off the wheel to hold forth about *Gammer Gurton's Needle*. I had the sense that my life could veer away in any direction, figuratively as well as literally.

I also liked the social mix of students. At Cambridge everyone was middle-class, trying to be middle-class or trying not to be. At London University the students came from all possible backgrounds, with very different approaches to everything. In my group was a surprisingly free-thinking nun, who wore a wimple and a full nun's rig. There were several ex-servicemen who had become interested in taking a degree while in the wartime forces. They had travelled all over the world. One or two were married. Another had spent his entire childhood in foster homes, was pleasantly good-humoured but quietly anti-semitic. They were all intelligent, which wasn't true of Cambridge undergraduates, and already had original ideas about the world. When I mentioned that I had been born in China and interned during the war they noted this in the way they would have reacted had I told them I was born in a North Sea trawler or a lighthouse.

The English course was interesting, but modern fiction played no part in it, and at the end of my first year I decided to leave Queen Mary College. My attempts to write a new experimental novel were a complete flop. I needed to get away from academic institutions, and I needed to be free of all financial dependence on my parents, a sentiment I am sure they shared. They were strongly opposed to my hopes of becoming a professional writer, and I found their hostility wearing. Through a Cambridge friend who was working for Benson's advertising agency in Kingsway, where Dorothy Sayers had worked and which housed the spiral staircase that appeared in one of her novels, I found a job as a novice copy-writer with a small London agency.

Like most people living in London for the first time, I spent many of my free hours visiting art galleries and museums, especially the National Gallery and the Tate, as well as the commercial galleries off Bond Street. Now and then there would be a small exhibition of new surrealist paintings – I remember Dalí at, I think, the Lefevre Gallery, and a show of new Magrittes. These sold for remarkably low prices, even the Dalís, but the surrealists had lost most of their prestige and appeal after the war. Their wayward imaginations seemed tame by comparison with the horrors of the Nazi death camps, and no one gave them credit for anticipating the pathological strains in the European mind that had propelled Hitler into power. There were very few surrealists in the Tate collection, and while I was interested in modern art as a whole, my imagination wasn't touched by cubism or abstract art, which seemed to be formal exercises confined to the artist's studio.

Today it seems to me that the works by modernist pioneers displayed in the Tate have begun to lose their lustre. Those landmark paintings by Picasso and Braque, Utrillo and Léger, Mondrian and Kandinsky appear smaller than they did fifty years ago. Their colour has faded, and they lack the imaginative bite that I felt when I first looked at them. At the same time I have to accept that my entire visual response to the world was kindled in those Millbank galleries I visited in my early twenties. Then, whenever I visited the Tate, I would always turn right into the modern rooms, and never left to the British art of the past four centuries. I admired Turner because he seemed to anticipate the Impressionists, but the Pre-Raphaelite painters, and Burne-Jones in particular, presented an airless and over-imagined realm as suffocating as the children's books I read uneasily as a boy. Today, my sense of direction has changed: whenever I enter the Tate I first turn left, and never right.

Surprisingly, given my passion for the new, I spent a huge amount of time in the National Gallery, and would often go every day. By a touching coincidence, my future partner Claire Walsh, then a hyper-bright 12-year-old Claire Churchill, would also visit the National Gallery, as part of her intellectual roaming around London. I wish I had seen her. Gallery tours are now part of every school curriculum, but in the early 1950s even the National Gallery would often seem deserted, and a visitor could be alone in a room filled with Rembrandts, a powerful charge to the imagination.

I am sure that a large part of the enduring mystery of the Renaissance masterpieces in the National Gallery was due to the absence of the explanatory matter that now drains away much of the strangeness and poetry of the Old Masters. I would stare at Crivelli's *Annunciation*, charmed by the peacocks, loaves of bread and other incongruous items, the passer-by reading a book on the bridge and the Virgin in her jewel box of a house. I was forced to use my own imagination to stitch these elements into a master narrative that made some kind of sense, rather than read an extended wall caption and be solemnly told that the peacock was a symbol of eternal life. Perish the thought, and let the exquisite bird be itself, and nothing more or less than itself. What could be more natural, and more mysterious, than a peacock and a loaf of bread appearing on the scene to celebrate the forthcoming birth of the Saviour?

Years later, standing in the Uffizi Gallery in Florence in front of another *Annunciation*, by Leonardo, I found my view blocked by a huge party of Japanese tourists. I wondered what they made of the religious paintings in the gallery, with their winged men kneeling in front of rather self-conscious young women. A few Japanese take the Latin mass, but most know nothing about the Christian myths, and the paintings must have seemed completely surrealist.

Then I realised what had drawn me to the National Gallery. There were very few surrealist paintings on display in London in the early 1950s. Colour printing was in its infancy, and there were few illustrated books at affordable prices. I had unconsciously done the only thing I could – I had turned the National Gallery into a virtual museum of surrealist art, and co-opted Leonardo, Raphael and Mantegna to become surrealist painters for me.

In 1955 there was a modest retrospective of Francis Bacon's paintings at the Institute of Contemporary Arts, followed in 1962 by a far larger retrospective at the Tate Gallery, which was a revelation to me. I still think of Bacon as the greatest painter of the post-war world. Sadly, when I met him in the 1980s I found, like many others before me, that he was not interested in receiving compliments or in talking about his own work. I suspect that he was still sensitive to charges of gratuitous violence and sensationalism that were levelled at him in the 1950s and 1960s. He chose as his official inter-viewer the art critic David Sylvester, who was careful to steer clear of the questions everyone was eager to hear answered, and only asked Bacon about his handling of space and other academic topics. In his replies Bacon adopted the same elliptical and evasive language, with the result that we know less about the motives of this extraordinary painter than we do of almost any other 20th-century artist. At least Crivelli's *Annunciation* in the 1950s was not screened behind endless lectures on Renaissance perspective and the fluctuating price of lapis lazuli.

Bacon's paintings were screams from the abattoir, cries from the execution pits of World War II. His deranged executives and his princes of death in their pontiffs' robes lacked all pity and remorse. His popes screamed because they knew there was no God. Bacon went even further than the surrealists, assuming our complicity in the mid-century's horrors. It was we who sat in those claustrophobic rooms, like TV hospitality suites in need of a coat of paint, under a naked light bulb that might signal the arrival of the dead, the only witnesses at our last interview.

Yet Bacon kept hope alive at a dark time, and looking at his paintings gave me a surge of confidence. I knew there was a link of some kind with the surrealists, with the dead doctors lying in their wooden chests in the dissecting room, with film noir and with the peacock and the loaf of bread in Crivelli's *Annunciation*. There were links to Hemingway and Camus and Nathanael West. A jigsaw inside my head was trying to assemble itself, but the picture when it finally emerged would appear in an unexpected place.

14

Vital Discoveries (1953)

Working as a copywriter at an advertising agency was not as glamorous or interesting as novels and films suggested. Most of it was a slog, a dull chore of writing booklets and copy for manuals. I needed the daylight to write my own fiction, so I took a job as a Covent Garden porter, working in the chrysanthemum department of a large wholesaler. We started early, at something like 6 o'clock, and were through by noon. When too many sleep-starved nights finally got to me, I sold encyclopaedias door to door, a job at which I was surprisingly successful, partly because the *Waverley Encyclopaedia* was the one I had read as a child in Shanghai – I knew it backwards and genuinely believed in it.

It was a fascinating time, roaming the Midland towns with my samples, living in shabby hotels among garment workers. A modest street of Victorian terraced houses would hold a universe of differences – cheerful teenage girls bringing up a brood of small children while the mother slumped in the kitchen watching TV among the clutter; religious fanatics with barely a stick of furniture and wary daughters who couldn't wait to grow up; a man so excited that I worked for a publisher that he propelled me into his living room and proudly showed me a piano whose keys were coloured and numbered, his 'revolutionary' system for teaching music that he wanted me to market for him – by way of proof, he whistled up the stairs and his amiable 13-year-old daughter came down and sat at the upright with her sheet music annotated like a candy bar, then solemnly played the Moonlight Sonata. I still see coloured stripes when I hear the melody, and taste sweetness on my lips.

Prosperity of a sort had reached the Midlands, and the early 1950s was on the cusp of social change. The poorer that people were, the keener they seemed to be to buy the encyclopaedia, and I often waived my commission (there was no salary) to secure for them the hours of intelligent pleasure I had known as a child. But the better-off residents, especially those working in the Coventry car plants, had moved beyond the hallowed notion of education as a gateway to success. Information came through advertising and the television set. They would show off their huge new screens, their wall-to-wall carpeting and their modern kitchens and bathrooms, taking it for granted that I was genuinely interested in these features, then politely decline the eight-volume *Waverley*. Consumerism provided all the bearings they needed in their lives.

Meanwhile, my writing was still stuck. I had sensibly

abandoned my efforts to go one better than *Finnegans Wake*, and knew that I wasn't muscular and morbid enough to emulate Hemingway. My problem was that I hadn't found a form that suited me. Popular fiction was too popular, and literary fiction too earnest. A spate of World War II memoirs and novels was being published, but surprisingly it never occurred to me to write a novel based on my own wartime experiences. Even the grim events I had witnessed as a child in Shanghai could never match the genocidal horrors of the Nazi death camps.

By now, seven or eight years after the war, I had begun to switch off my memories of Shanghai. Very few people had shared my experiences, and the European war was still everywhere around us in a hundred bomb sites. I had always detested nostalgia, and the attempt by British politicians of all parties to assert Britain's importance in the world, when in reality we were nearly bankrupt, by harping on our wartime role and our pre-war empire, reminded me of the danger of dwelling too much in the past. The Shanghai years would never return, and it unsettled me whenever I met friends of my parents and former Lunghua internees who were detached from the present and living entirely within a cocoon of China memories.

Flying still interested me, and I began to notice advertisements for short-service commissions in the RAF. The flight training was in Canada, an added attraction. My years in Lunghua had exempted me from National Service, and as an officer I would be able to leave the service if I was reassigned to ground duties, as happened to so many pilots and navigators. A change of scene, from grey and over-crowded London to the vast spaces of central Canada, would give me time to think and with any luck be a new spur to my imagination. I was still only 23, but my career as a novelist showed no signs of ever beginning.

I signed on at the RAF recruitment offices in Kingsway, passed the assessment tests at RAF Hornchurch, near Dagenham, and started my three-month basic training at Kirton in Lindsey, in Lincolnshire. I enjoyed my time there, a mix of army-style drill and square-bashing, basic navigation and meteorology, weapons training with the Lee-Enfield rifle, Smith & Wesson revolver and Sten machine gun (I turned out to be a fairly good shot), lessons in officers' mess etiquette (we would be Britain's ambassadors around the world as well as becoming nuclear bomber pilots), and experts at self-diagnosing the first symptoms of VD, thanks to hours of instructional films that gave a rather odd impression of our future role as serving officers of the Queen.

In the autumn of 1954 we sailed for Canada on one of the Empress liners, and then spent a month at an RCAF base near London, Ontario, not far from Detroit and Niagara Falls. The intention was to 'culturally relocate' us within the North American way of life, and wean us off the enticements of cricket, warm beer and toad-in-the-hole. Needless to say, we were all eager to embrace the North American way of life from the second we stepped off the Empress boat. Canadians were generous and hospitable, without any of the rough edges that can make America jar. The country was vast and sparsely populated, and virtually under a blanket of snow for six months of the year. The Canadians had the natural warmth towards strangers of a desert people.

We arrived at our training base in Moose Jaw, Saskatchewan, as the first snow was falling, and I think it was still falling when I left the following spring. NATO pilot training took place in Canada as part of the country's contribution to the alliance, but a wilderness of ice and snow was not the best location for a flying school. The fierce isolation of the Canadian winter, and the white world that surrounded the airbase ten miles from Moose Jaw, meant that for long periods we had nothing to do but sit in the flight rooms, reading magazines and watching the snow fall on the buried runways. Now and then a moose would leap the perimeter fence and gallop off into the mist. In the very comfortable mess, virtually a four-star hotel, I would sit by the picture windows and watch the snow carried horizontally by the icy wind. Walking to the mess from our barracks, I would sometimes find small contact lenses on my cheeks – ice dislodged from my eyeballs when I blinked. We lived on turkey, waffles and ice cream, and drank the bar out of its bourbon and gin. There was no taboo about flying and drinking – one of my Canadian instructors always boarded our plane with a cigar and two bottles of beer.

Then the weather would clear, brilliant blue skies above the silent snow, and we would get in a few days of pilot training. I enjoyed flying the heavy Harvard T-6, with its huge radial engine, retractable undercarriage and variable-pitch propeller, but the training was continually hampered by the weather. Ice crystals in the air produced extraordinary atmospheric effects, such as the triple suns that would blaze through the frozen haze. The British trainees were happy to loaf around, but the French and Turkish trainees demanded to be sent home. They were older and senior in rank to many of the RCAF instructors. At one point the French staged a mutiny, refusing to eat the food served in the mess, which they claimed was fit only for children. The Turks, all experienced army officers, declined to accept orders from any RCAF instructor junior to them. A senior French liaison officer had to be flown in from Ottawa, and was told to climb up the nearest flagpole.

With a great deal of time on my hands, I wrote a few short stories and tried to find enough reading matter to keep me going. The regional newspapers carried no international news and consisted of nothing except reports of curling and ice hockey matches. Magazines such as *Time* were regarded as intensely highbrow and were difficult to get hold of in Moose Jaw, which was then a dead-end town with two filling stations and a bus depot. Its main function was to supply tractor parts to the huge wheat farms that covered the whole of Saskatchewan. Most of the paperbacks in the bus depot were popular thrillers and detective stories, but there was one type of fiction that occupied a lot of space on the book racks. This was science fiction, then enjoying its great post-war boom.

Up to that point I had read very little science fiction, apart from the Buck Rogers and Flash Gordon comic strips of my Shanghai childhood. I would later realise that most professional s-f writers, British and American, were keen fans from their early teens, and many began their careers writing for the fanzines (amateur magazines produced by enthusiasts) and attending conventions. I was one of the very few who came to science fiction at a relatively late age. By the mid 1950s there were some twenty commercial s-f magazines on monthly sale in America and Canada, and the best of these were in the Moose Jaw magazine racks.

Some, like *Astounding Science Fiction*, the front runner in both sales and prestige within the field, were heavily committed to space travel and tales of a hard-edged technological future. Almost all the stories were set in spaceships or on alien planets in the very far future. These planet yarns, in which most of the characters wore military uniform, soon bored me. The forerunners of *Star Trek*, they described an American imperium colonising the entire universe, which they turned into a cheerful, optimistic hell, a 1950s American suburb paved with good intentions and populated by Avon ladies in spacesuits. Eerily, this may prove to be an accurate prophecy.

Luckily, there were other magazines like *Galaxy* and *Fantasy & Science Fiction*, where the short stories were set in the present or very near future, extrapolating social and political trends already evident in the years after the war. The dangers to a docile public of television, advertising and the American media landscape were their terrain. They looked searchingly at the abuses of psychiatry and at politics conducted as a branch of advertising. Many of the stories were droll and pessimistic, with a surface of dry wit that hid a quite downbeat message.

These I seized on and began to devour. Here was a form of fiction that was actually about the present day, and often as elliptical and ambiguous as Kafka. It recognised a world dominated by consumer advertising, of democratic government mutating into public relations. This was a world of cars, offices, highways, airlines and supermarkets that we actually lived in, but which was completely missing from almost all serious fiction. No one in a novel by Virginia Woolf ever filled up the petrol tank of her car. No one in Sartre or Thomas Mann ever paid for a haircut. No one in Hemingway's post-war novels ever worried about the effects of prolonged exposure to the threat of nuclear war. The very notion was ludicrous, as absurd then as it seems now. Writers of so-called serious fiction shared one dominant characteristic – their fiction was first and foremost about themselves. The 'self' lay at the heart of modernism, but now had a powerful rival, the everyday world, which was just as much a psychological construct, and just as prone to mysterious and often psychopathic impulses. It was this rather sinister realm, a consumer society that might decide to go on a day trip to another Auschwitz and another Hiroshima, that science fiction was exploring.

Above all, the s-f genre had a huge vitality. Without thinking up a plan of action, I decided that this was a field I should enter. I could see that here was a literary form that placed a premium on originality, and gave a great deal of latitude to its writers, many of whom had their own trademark styles and approaches. I felt too that for all its vitality, magazine science fiction was limited by its 'what if?' approach, and that the genre was ripe for change, if not outright takeover. I was more interested in a 'what now?' approach. After weekend trips across the border I could see that both Canada and the USA were changing rapidly, and that change would in time reach even Britain. I would interiorise science fiction, looking for the pathology that underlay the consumer society, the TV landscape and the nuclear arms race, a vast untouched continent of fictional possibility. Or so I thought, staring at the silent airfield, with its empty runways that stretched into a snow-blanched infinity.

In early spring, when the last of the snow was falling, we were told that our flight training would be transferred back to England (within a year RCAF Moose Jaw ceased to be a NATO training centre). By this time I was confident that my career as a writer was about to begin. I had written several s-f stories, which had flowed quickly from my pen, and there was a queue of others waiting in my mind. I enjoyed flying, but months in an isolated training base in Scotland or the north of England would postpone everything I planned.

Accordingly, I resigned my commission, and was soon installed in my tiny couchette on the Canadian Pacific Railway train to Toronto, a long journey of endless lakes and pine forests that I spent with pad and pencil. In a real sense I wrote my way across Canada, and then across the Atlantic to England. On arrival I was sent to RAF High Wycombe, where RAF personnel were demobilised.

It was a cold spring, and we sat in an unheated barrack room on the edge of a disused airfield, waiting to be called by the two flight lieutenants who processed our papers. As the days passed I would strike up the acquaintance of a V-bomber navigator cashiered for some mess irregularity, or a pilot who had damaged the undercarriage of his jet fighter by hitting one too many landing lights. Then 'Robertson' or 'Groundwater' would be called out, a half-finished *Times* crossword would be pressed into my hands, and my new companions would vanish for ever.

Since my papers had to come from Canada, I spent several weeks at RAF High Wycombe, a gloomy place that managed a convincing impersonation of the end of the world. But I have fond memories of it; firstly, because it was there that I wrote my first s-f story to be published, and secondly because I was looking forward to seeing Mary Matthews, whom I had met in a Notting Hill hotel a month before I joined the RAF. We had exchanged a few letters while I was in Canada, but I had no idea if she would still be there.

15

Miracles of Life (1955)

As soon as I left RAF High Wycombe I travelled straight to London, and booked myself into the hotel near Ladbroke Grove where Mary and I had first met. Friends had brought us together at a party held in the large communal garden behind Stanley Crescent, an untended wilderness that I remember as a cross between Arcadia and a jungle-warfare training range. Today this entire area is dominated by bankers, hedge-fund managers and television executives, but in the 1950s it was a warren of shabby boarding houses and one-room flats occupied by jobless ex-servicemen, part-time prostitutes, divorcees with small children living on handouts from their relatives; in short the flotsam of down-at-heel post-war England who could not even afford to be poor.

Yet respectability kept breaking through, and young professionals were already beginning to infiltrate the area. Mary Matthews was one of them. Arriving in London to take up her job as a secretary at the *Daily Express*, she moved into the Stanley Crescent Hotel because it advertised a handbasin with hot and cold running water in every room, a remarkable feature at the time, and as much a sign of middle-class success as a second bathroom in a suburban house today.

Yet this was Christie country, and Rillington Place (later renamed), where the ghastly John Christie committed his murders, was only a few hundred yards away. Back in 1953, soon after my meeting with Peter Wyngarde at the Mitre in Holland Park Avenue, I was walking up Ladbroke Grove when I found a huge crowd outside the police station. They filled the side street, watching the entrance to the car park behind the station. A police car approached, siren ringing, followed by a police van. The crowd drew back, leaving a woman in a red coat standing in the middle of the side street. The constables guarding the car park entrance made no attempt to move her, and she stood her ground, watched admiringly by the crowd as the police car and van swerved at speed through the gates.

The woman in the red coat was the sister of Timothy Evans, a mentally retarded friend of Christie who had been charged with the murder of his son and hanged in 1950. In fact, Christie had murdered the infant, and was himself hanged in 1953. Evans, too late, received a posthumous pardon in 1966. I can still remember the woman in the red coat, and her implacable gaze as she stared at the police van. Inside was John Christie, a now-deranged figure who had just been arrested for the murders he had committed at Rillington Place.

My wife, Mary Ballard, in 1956.

I had originally moved to the Stanley Crescent Hotel after being driven out of South Kensington, when the weekly rent for my room in Onslow Gardens rose from 36 shillings a week to two guineas. South Kensington was beginning to stir, as old money that had retreated to the countryside for the duration of the war began to return to its stucco villas. I preferred Notting Hill, for its general raffishness and unexpected delights, chief among them Mary Matthews.

When I first met Mary, shortly before joining the RAF, she was working as a secretary for Charles Wintour (father of Anna, the 'tyrant' of *Vogue*; he later became editor of the *Evening Standard*, but was then a senior editor at the *Daily Express*). Born in 1930, Mary was the daughter of Dorothy Vernon and her husband Arthur Matthews, who were well-to-do landowners in Stone, Staffordshire. Mary's father served in the Honourable Artillery Company during the Great War and was invalided out. At the time I met them in 1955 they were living in a modest cottage in Dyserth, a village near Prestatyn in north Wales. They grew their own vegetables and had a simple and pleasantly provincial life together. Like Mary and her two sisters, Peggy and Betty, they were extremely generous people with strong moral principles.

I think Mary was the most adventurous of the sisters, the youngest but the most ambitious, and the only one who wanted to live and work in London. She was enormously optimistic, and confident that anything was possible if enough willpower was brought to bear. She was tall, with a striking figure and great presence, a woman whom men immediately noticed. In many ways she remained a girl from the Potteries, and at times appeared to be a dizzy brunette, something of an act, as she was quick-witted. All my men-friends liked her enormously, and she was generally popular at the *Express*. She had enjoyed a very active social life in Stone, a world of big houses, prosperous farmers driving

Armstrong Siddeleys, lavish private dances and several very dashing suitors.

What she saw in me I still find it difficult to work out. I was probably rather 'lost' in her eyes, but she knew that I was ambitious. I lived on the floor below her in a wing of the hotel, and I worked hard at making myself useful. We began to spend increasing amounts of time in the pubs along the Portobello Road, getting pleasantly tight together. For some reason I delayed telling her about my Shanghai background, which I was afraid might appear a little like a criminal record. In some half-conscious sense it was. Mary was not impressed to hear that I was joining the RAF, but her eyes widened a little when I said that I was writing a novel, a rare phenomenon among the point-to-points and hunt balls. 'Have you nearly finished?' she asked me, to which I replied, truthfully: 'No, I've nearly begun.' She saw the joke, but also the serious point lurking somewhere behind it.

What rather raised me in Mary's eyes was the modest part I played in the Mrs Shanahan incident. This on-and-off prostitute lived in a room above Mary with her 7-year-old daughter. When times were low she would bring back customers from the Portobello pubs, for some reason always large and tired men who would climb the stairs past Mary's door as if on the way to the gallows. What disturbed us was the presence of the daughter, who would be dressed in a grey silk Marie Antoinette dress and hat, carrying a little baroque umbrella. Blank-faced and unsmiling, she would remain in the Shanahan room while business was transacted.

I still prided myself on the thought that I had seen every-thing in Shanghai, but this completely shook me. What on earth did the daughter do in her Petit Trianon outfit while her mother and the customer had sex? Did she take part? I prayed not, and I guessed that all she did was watch, or sit behind a curtain, twiddling her umbrella. Mary didn't care what she did, but wanted the whole horror stopped. She bought little presents for the child, which made Mrs Shanahan effusively grateful, and she was overly keen to be our friends, forever offering to cook meals for us; she told Mary that I was far too thin. I suspect that a wall divided her mind, separating her affectionate, everyday life with her daughter from the spectral moments imposed by neces-sity. Pressed by Mary, I spoke to the manager, a tired Pole exhausted by climbing the stairs to badger his tenants for the rent. I threatened to call the police, something I probably would never have done, I regret to say. The next day Mrs Shanahan and her daughter had gone, and Mary assumed, with her good nature and high principles, that this was a happy ending. I hope it was.

When I left High Wycombe, the RAF now behind me, and booked into the Stanley Crescent Hotel I found that nothing had changed. The same tired tenants were still there, one of the lost tribes of Britain's post-war world, among them a retired RAF squadron leader and his very posh wife, Peta, who was always boasting in a loud voice that she had 'checked out on twin-engines' (was authorised to fly twin-engined aircraft) before her husband. To her annoyance, he was never able to pay the rent, and I think she knew that her husband had given up hope. The Polish manager would linger in the breakfast room (breakfast was never served, except to cash-on-the-nail tenants), waiting until Peta was in full twin-engined flight with another guest, and then step up to her, saying in a loud voice: 'You are three weeks behind with your rent, Mrs...' Peta would flounce away, angry that I had witnessed this little humiliation. Only a few years earlier they had been stationed in Cyprus, with a large house and servants. She was lost in post-war England, but a perfect symbol of it.

There was a wartime Navy lieutenant who had captained a motor torpedo boat. He lived in one room with his amiable wife and baby daughter, and spent his time building model seacraft. Some years earlier, he had damaged his brain by diving into the wrong end of a swimming pool. I became good friends with him, and would help carry the picnic equipment to Kensington Gardens and watch him sail his models in the Round Pond. All these people, like myself, would have been classed as misfits, casualties of war who had lost their way in the peace, but at least we all accepted each other and there was never any rivalry. Today that one-star hotel would be full of financial hustlers, celebrity hunters, people with huge expectations and aware that a lack of any real talent was no handicap to success. Any novice writer would flee in horror. I remember the old Stanley Crescent Hotel with affection.

Above all, of course, because Mary was still there. I left my suitcase in my old room, luckily vacant, and knocked on the door of Mary's room. It was opened by a middle-aged woman in a nursing sister's uniform. For a few seconds my heart died, and I realised why I had left the Air Force and travelled all the way from Moose Jaw. Then I learned that Mary had moved to a larger room on the first floor.

I think we were surprised, a little wary but almost relieved to see each other again.

Mary lent me her typewriter, and over the next few weeks I typed out all the stories I had written on the way back to England. She read them very carefully, was clearly impressed by them, and not in the least put off by the fact that they were science fiction, which she had never read. She strongly urged me to press on, though most of her friends regarded science fiction as beyond the pale. But she sensed that there was something original and fresh about this apparently modest genre, that it was optimistic and positive, and drew on qualities within my mind that had been repressed since my arrival in England. The wilder side of my imagination was its strength, and I needed to tap that, at least for the time being. From the very beginning she was convinced that I would be a success as a writer.

Here she differed completely from my parents, who were convinced that I would be a failure. Looking back, I am puzzled by their lack of support, but they may have believed that the wilder side of my imagination needed to be repressed, not released. Mary tried to be charitable, but she disliked my parents. As it happened, we saw little of them in the coming years, and I now had all the emotional support I needed.

Mary listened for hours as I described the kind of fiction I wanted to write, urging me to keep up a steady flow of short stories and to ignore the strong hostility they provoked from the s-f fans within the field. I submitted my stories to the American s-f magazines that I had read in Moose Jaw, but all came back to me, usually with very dismissive rejection notes, which revealed the narrowness of mind that lurks behind American exuberance. A fierce orthodoxy ruled, and any attempt to enlarge the scope of traditional science fiction was regarded as conspiratorial and underhand.

In due course Mary became pregnant, and we were married in September 1955. Mary's family, my parents and sister, and a few friends attended the church service, which moved me deeply. Three of us, in a sense, were being married – Mary, I and our unborn child. I took the ceremony very seriously, though not for religious reasons. My life had been witness to wars and destruction, to erosion and entropy, capped by two years in the dissecting room at Cambridge, paring down the cadavers as if death itself was not final enough, and the remains of these human beings needed to be further diminished. Now, for the first time, I had helped to create something, almost out of nothing, an intact and growing creature that would emerge as a living being. Mary was three months pregnant when we married, and I would lie beside her, touching the swelling of her womb, willing on this little visitor from beyond time and space. Creation on the grandest scale was taking place under the warmth of my hand.

I remember the wedding ceremony as a slightly disjointed affair. The respective in-laws had not met each other, and the old tribal defensiveness showed itself. Waiting for the clergyman to arrive, I turned to my father in the pew behind me and asked if I should leave a donation 'for the poor of the parish'. He replied, jovially: 'You are the poor of the parish.' He and my mother enjoyed the joke.

Strictly speaking, this was true. I made a small income writing freelance advertising copy and direct-mail letters for an agency I knew, but I needed a full-time job to support us now that Mary had given up her post at the *Express*. Luckily I had begun to sell my short stories to the two English science fiction magazines, *Science Fantasy* and *New Worlds*, and the first was published in 1956, a signal moment in any writer's career, especially that of a late starter like myself.

The editor, E.J. Carnell, was a thoughtful and likeable man

who worked in a pleasant basement office near the Strand. The walls were hung with posters of s-f films and magazine covers that together conveyed a rather conventional view of the nature of science fiction. In private, though, once he was away from the old-guard fans, Carnell told me that science fiction needed to change if it was to remain at the cutting edge of the future. He urged me not to imitate the American writers, and to concentrate on what I termed 'inner space', psychological tales close in spirit to the surrealists. All this was anathema to the American editors, who continued to reject my fiction.

But we listened in 1957 to the radio call sign of Sputnik 1, an urgent wake-up call from the next world and the dawn of the Space Age. For the s-f traditionalists, Sputnik 1 confirmed all their most precious dreams, but I was sceptical. To hold its readers' imaginations, I believed, science fiction needed to be the harbinger of the new, not a reminder of the old. Soon after, sure enough, science fiction went into a steep decline in the United States, from which it didn't recover until the advent of *Star Wars* decades later.

Aware that I needed a job, with a wife and baby son to support, Carnell arranged for me to get an editorial post on one of the trade journals published by his parent company. There were always vacancies because the firm paid so little to its employees, from the editors down. Colleagues would go out for a packet of cigarettes and never return. After six months I too moved on to a better-paid post as deputy editor of the weekly journal *Chemistry & Industry*, published by the Society of Chemical Industry in Belgrave Square.

After our wedding, Mary and I lived, first, in a flat in Barrowgate Road, Chiswick, and then for several years in a larger flat in Heathcote Road, St Margarets, near Twickenham. Our son, James, was born in the Chiswick Maternity Hospital, part of the NHS, but a strangely penal institution that enshrined then-fashionable views about the post-natal care of mothers and their babies. There was no question of fathers being present at the delivery; we were told to stay at home until called. When I arrived soon after the birth I found Mary in a ward with five other mothers, all weeping as they listened to their babies desperately crying in a separate ward across the corridor. Mother and child were only united during feeding times, set out in an inflexible rota. When I protested I was told that it would be better if I left the hospital.

Our daughters, Fay and Beatrice, were born in 1957 and 1959. Both were home deliveries, from the heart of a warm domestic nest, and in which I actively participated, almost shouldering the midwives aside. In the untidy but blissful bed where our two daughters were conceived they were in due course born, surrounded by Mary's sisters and close friends. I was profoundly moved as Fay's head emerged into the midwife's waiting hands, just as I was two years later when Bea arrived in the same bed. Far from being young, as young as a human being can be, they seemed immensely old, their foreheads and features streamlined by time, as archaic and smooth as the heads of pharaohs in Egyptian sculpture, as if they had travelled an immense distance to find their parents. Then, in a second, they became young and were carried off by the midwife and Mary's sister. Only a few minutes earlier I had been kneeling beside the bed, pressing back Mary's large and bursting piles, and now I lay beside her as she smiled, embraced me and fell asleep. I wept steadily through both these deliveries, the greatest mystery that life can offer, and I regret that so few babies, if any, are born today in their own homes.

Once the children arrived our domestic world became chaotic. Mary was never much of a housekeeper, but became a kind of earth mother, sitting up in bed and breastfeeding a baby while sipping a glass of wine and arguing in a strong voice about some topic of the day with two of my men-friends. One of the Twickenham GPs who looked after her became quite besotted, and was happy to be called at any hour of the day or night to sit on the bed beside her, a romantic infatuation that she thought hilarious, even as she was leading the poor man towards disciplinary proceedings at the General Medical Council.

Despite the pressures of her new job as homemaker, wife and mother of three, Mary tried to read everything I wrote. For the first time I had someone who believed in me, and was prepared to back that belief by putting up with a rather modest life. She was always confident that one day I would be a success, which seemed unlikely in the late 1950s, when science fiction was generally regarded as not much better than the comic strips.

In 1960, as our toddlers found their legs, we decided we needed a home with a garden, and bought a small house in Shepperton, where I live to this day. I think I chose Shepperton because of its film studios, which gave it a slightly raffish air. Mary assumed that we would stay there for no more than six months, but three years later, after the success of *The Drowned World*, there still seemed little hope of moving, which I think depressed her, as did the literary world as a whole.

We began to meet other writers, both in and out of the s-f world, and she realised that even successful writers in England had rather humdrum lives. Publishers' parties and writers' boozy blow-outs in Clapham flats did not compare with the life of hunt balls and fast cars she had left behind in Stone. I am sure that we would have eventually moved to a detached house with a big garden in Barnes or Wimbledon, but even that would have been very tame compared with the world of well-to-do farmers and landowners, Lagondas and lavish dances.

All the same, I hope that her years here were happy. I tried to share the load, and enjoyed every minute I spent with the children, watching them create their own universes out of a few toys, treats and games. I knew that I was enjoying a family life I had never really known, even in pre-war

Shanghai. I had rarely seen my parents in a relaxed, domestic mood. Their lives were too busy, and everything took place in the silent presence of Chinese servants and the bored White Russian nannies. Our home in Shepperton, by contrast, was a chaotic, friendly brawl, as a naked parent dripping from the bath broke up a squabble between the girls over a favourite crayon, while their brother triumphantly strutted in his mother's damp footprints. Mayhem ruled.

To give Mary a break, I often heaped the three toddlers into their huge pram, a stretch limousine of the perambulator world, and would push them down to the splash meadow a few hundred yards from our house. The river Ash, little more than a stream, emerged from a culvert and crossed the road, flanked by a pedestrian bridge where an appreciative crowd would lean on the rail and watch unsuspecting motorists strand their stalled cars in the stream. The scene in *Genevieve*, where the antique car is stranded in the village pond, was filmed here. My children loved to watch the whole hilarious spectacle, chortling and stamping as a nonplussed driver finally lowered his feet into the water, under the gaze of a sinister yokel and his offspring.

We spent hours with little fish nets, hunting for shrimps, which were always taken home in jam jars and watched as they refused to cooperate and gave up the ghost. Fay and Bea were fascinated by the daisies that seemed to grow underwater when the stream rose to flood the meadow.

Shepperton Studios were easy to enter in those wonderful summers nearly fifty years ago, and I would take the children past the sound stages to the field where unwanted props were left to the elements: figureheads of sailing ships, giant chess-pieces, half an American car, stairways that led up to the sky and amazed my three infants. And their father: days of wonder that I wish had lasted for ever.

I thought of my children then, and still think of them, as miracles of life, and I dedicate this autobiography to them.

16

This is Tomorrow (1956)

In 1956, the year that I published my first short story, I visited a remarkable exhibition at the Whitechapel Art Gallery, This is Tomorrow. Recently I told Nicholas Serota, director of the Tate and a former director of the Whitechapel, that I thought This is Tomorrow was the most important event in the visual arts in Britain until the opening of Tate Modern, and he did not disagree.

Among its many achievements, This is Tomorrow is generally thought of as the birthplace of pop art. A dozen teams, involving an architect, a painter and sculptor, each designed and built an installation that would embody their vision of the future. The participants included the artist Richard Hamilton, who displayed his collage *Just what is it that makes today's homes so different, so appealing?*, in my judgement the greatest ever work of pop art. Another of the teams brought together the sculptor Eduardo Paolozzi, and the architects Peter and Alison Smithson, who constructed a basic unit of human habitation in what would be left of the world after nuclear war. Their terminal hut, as I thought of it, stood on a patch of sand, on which were laid out the basic implements that modern man would need to survive: a power tool, a bicycle wheel and a pistol.

The overall effect of This is Tomorrow was a revelation to me, and a vote of confidence, in effect, in my choice of science fiction. The Whitechapel exhibition, and especially the Hamilton and Paolozzi exhibits, created a huge stir in the British art world. At the time the artists most in favour with the Arts Council, the British Council and the academic critics of the day were Henry Moore, Barbara Hepworth, John Piper and Graham Sutherland, who together formed a closed fine art world largely preoccupied with formalist experiment. The light of everyday reality never shone into the aseptic whiteness of their studio-bound imaginations.

This is Tomorrow opened all the doors and windows onto the street. The show leaned a little on Hollywood and American science fiction; Hamilton had got hold of Robby the Robot from the film *Forbidden Planet*. But for the first time the visitor to the Whitechapel saw the response of imaginations tuned to the visual culture of the street, to advertising, road signs, films and popular magazines, to the design of packaging and consumer goods, an entire universe that we moved through in our everyday lives but which rarely appeared in the approved fine art of the day.

Hamilton's *Just what is it...?* depicted a world entirely constructed from popular advertising, and was a convincing vision of the future that lay ahead – the muscleman husband and his stripper wife in their suburban home, the consumer goods, such as the tin of ham, regarded as ornaments in their own right, the notion of the home as a prime selling point and sales aid for the consumer society. We are what we sell and buy.

In Paolozzi's display, the power tool laid on the post-nuclear sand was not just a portable device for drilling holes but a symbolic object with almost magical properties. If the future was to be built of anything, it would be from a set of building blocks provided by consumerism. An advertisement for a new cake mix contained the codes that defined a mother's relationship to her children, imitated all over our planet.

This is Tomorrow convinced me that science fiction was far closer to reality than the conventional realist novel of the day, whether the angry young men with their grudges and grouses, or novelists such as Anthony Powell and C.P. Snow. Above all, science fiction had a huge vitality that had bled away from the modernist novel. It was a visionary engine that created a new future with every revolution, a hot rod accelerating away from the reader, propelled by an exotic literary fuel as rich and dangerous as anything that drove the surrealists.

If pop art and surrealism were a huge encouragement, my work at *Chemistry & Industry* kept me up to the mark about the latest scientific discoveries. An established science magazine receives a steady flow of press releases, conference reports, annual bulletins from leading research laboratories around the world and publications put out by UN scientific bodies and organisations such as Atoms for Peace. I feasted on all this material, the accounts of new psychoactive drugs, nuclear weapons research, the applications of the latest-generation computers.

For several years I commuted to Belgrave Square, first from Twickenham and then from Shepperton, a long journey that left me too tired to write, except at weekends. After being cooped up all day with the children, Mary needed to breathe. I remember her saying when I reached home at 7.30 and was pouring a stiff gin and tonic: 'Are we going out? I can call the babysitter.' I thought: Out? I've been out. But we would go down to one of the pubs on the river-bank, and she would come alive when I bought a sandwich and threw bread to the swans.

In 1960, sadly for himself and his family, the editor of *Chemistry & Industry*, Bill Dick, killed himself with a gas poker and a plastic bag. He had been the once celebrated editor of the science magazine *Discovery*, but had become an argumentative alcoholic. After his death I was left alone to produce the magazine, and adjusted my time so that I could write in the office. My one piece of out-and-out commercial fiction, *The Wind from Nowhere*, was written straight onto the typewriter during a fortnight's holiday in 1961, and was published by an American paperback firm, Berkley Books. I received an advance of $1000, which seemed a fortune. I celebrated by moving from the 3/6 (three shillings and sixpence) lunch menu at the Swan pub in Knightsbridge to the 4/6 menu, an extravagance that alarmed the waitresses, to whom I had proudly shown a photograph of my three children. It is easy to forget how thin was the line between poverty and bare survival.

In 1963 *The Drowned World* was successfully published, and with Mary's encouragement I gave up my job at *Chemistry & Industry* and became a full-time writer. Despite the many editions of *The Drowned World*, this was a huge gamble, and I'm grateful and impressed that Mary urged me to take it. The novel was published all over the world, but the amounts of money forthcoming were modest.

Victor Gollancz, the patriarch of English publishing, paid me an advance of £100, barely enough to keep a family afloat for a month. When Gollancz took me out to lunch at The Ivy and I saw the prices on the menu I was tempted to say: I'll have nothing to eat, and just take the cash. But I knew that being lunched by Gollancz was a significant honour. He had dominated London publishing throughout the 1930s and 1940s, and had a huge influence on literary editors and readers. As we sat down in The Ivy he boomed in his loud voice: 'Interesting novel, *The Drowned World*. Of course, you stole it all from Conrad.' The Ivy was a haunt of senior journalists, and I saw heads turning. I thought: My God, this grand old man is going to sink my career before it's launched. As it happens, I had not read anything by Conrad at the time, though I soon made up for this.

My first decade as a writer coincided with a period of sustained change in England, as well as in the USA and Europe. The mood of post-war depression had begun to lift, and the death of Stalin eased international tensions, despite the Soviet development of the H-bomb. Cheap jet travel arrived with the Boeing 707, and the consumer society, already well established in America, began to appear in Britain. Change was in the air, affecting the nation's psychology for good or bad. Change was what I wrote about, especially the hidden agendas for change that people were already exposing. Invisible persuaders were manipulating politics and the consumer market, affecting habits and assumptions in ways that few people fully realised.

It seemed to me that psychological space, what I termed 'inner space', was where science fiction should be heading. But I met tremendous opposition. The editors of the American s-f magazines were nervous of their readers, and would refuse to accept a story if it was set in the present day, a sure sign that something subversive was going on. It was a curious paradox that science fiction, devoted to change and the new, was emotionally tied to the status quo and the old.

While I was at *Chemistry & Industry* I would regularly meet my fellow writer Michael Moorcock, who later took over Carnell's magazines when he retired. We had spirited arguments at the Swan in Knightsbridge over the direction science fiction should take. Moorcock was a highly intelligent and warm-hearted man, who embraced change and became a vocal spokesman for the New Wave, as the avantgarde wing of science fiction was known. What I admired most about Moorcock was that he was a complete professional, and had been since the age of 16, writing whatever he needed to write in order to make a living but always imposing his own vision. Daniel Defoe would have approved of him, and Dr Johnson. Moorcock was extremely well read – in fact, I sometimes think that he has read everything – but has kept his popular touch. He is writing for his readers, not for himself. I once said to him that I wanted to write for the sort of s-f magazine that was sold on news-stands, and bought by passers-by along with a copy of *Vogue* and the *New Statesman*, all hot from the street. Moorcock completely agreed.

Moving on the fringes of literary London for four decades, I have been constantly struck by how few of our literary writers are aware that their poor sales might be the result of their modest concern for their readers. B.S. Johnson, a thoroughly unpleasant figure who treated his sweet wife abominably, was forever telephoning and buttonholing me at literary parties, trying to enlist me in his campaign to persuade publishers to pay a higher royalty to their authors. At one point, when he was far gone in bitterness over his minuscule sales, he suggested we should demand a starting royalty of 50 per cent. Sadly, he was one of those literary writers who receive a glowing review in the *Times Literary Supplement*, believe every word of praise and imagine that it will ensure them a prosperous career, when in fact such a review is no more than the literary world's equivalent of 'Darling, you were wonderful…'

I had many reservations about science fiction as a whole, but the early 1960s were an exciting time. It was possible to have a short story in every issue of a magazine, each one exploring a new idea, a superb training ground. Too many writers today have to start their careers by writing novels, long before they are ready. I thought then, and still think, that in many ways science fiction was the true literature of the 20th century, with a vast influence on film, television, advertising and consumer design. Science fiction is now the only place where the future survives, just as television costume dramas are the only place where the past survives.

Apart from my friendship with Moorcock and his wife Hilary, I had few contacts with other writers. I went to the world s-f convention held in London in 1957, but the Americans were hard to take, and most of the British fans were worse. In Paris science fiction was popular among leading writers and film-makers like Robbe-Grillet and Resnais, and I assumed that I would find their counterparts in London, a huge error. Today's s-f enthusiasts are an entirely different breed, however. Many have university degrees, have read Joyce and Nabokov and seen *Alphaville*, and can place science fiction within a larger literary context. Yet curiously, science fiction itself is now in steep decline, and there may well be a moral there.

The first English novelist I met and got to know closely was Kingsley Amis. He had reviewed *The Drowned World* in extremely generous terms in the *Observer*, and was the first to introduce me to an audience beyond science fiction. He was then at the peak of his *Lucky Jim* fame, a highly intelligent, witty and glamorous figure who was pleasantly affable to anyone whose writing he liked. He reviewed science fiction in an open-minded way, maintaining that the best of the genre deserved to be taken seriously in the same way as jazz at its best.

After Victor Gollancz's death Amis joined Jonathan Cape, then the most fashionable publishing house in London, and effectively took me with him. Cape published me for the next twenty years, in some ways a mixed blessing. I knew Amis closely from 1962 to 1966, and often had lunch with him in Soho. He was a great drinking companion – the food served at Manzi's or Bertorelli's was little more than an appetiser for the real sustenance in the form of numerous bottles of claret. He was a great raconteur and brilliant mimic with a number of set-piece performances, such as President Roosevelt's wartime short-wave broadcasts, with isolated phrases like 'arsenal of democracy' and 'tanks, guns, planes' emerging from a blare of static.

Amis had just freed himself from his teaching post at Cambridge, and was in very good humour, but sadly this darkened over the next ten years as he grew dissatisfied with everything. I think he knew that his first book had been his best, and this led to heavier and heavier drinking, coupled with a certain social stiffness. Where once he was happy to drink beer in pubs, he now insisted on going to hotels, where he would order pink gins in an over-elaborate way.

By the last years of his life his hates were in full flow – Americans, Jews, the French and their entire culture, hippies and, for some unfathomable reason, Brigid Brophy. In the 1970s we once looked down during lunch from a window of the Café Royal at a protest march going along Regent Street. Amis began to tremble and shake. 'Jim, what are they? What *are* they?' He was almost speechless as he surveyed the column of cheerful young people with their anti-nuclear banners. To be fair to Amis, he had been through the war, and served in the army in northern Europe. While he had never taken part in combat, he told me, he had seen plenty of bodies by the roadside as the British forces advanced, and felt that he knew far more about the realities of war and peace than the soft-cheeked protesters in the street below us.

Amis disliked literary pretension (as he saw it) of any kind and was a remarkably astute judge of fiction, which I can say even though he later disliked a good part of my own writing. He believed in the 19th-century virtues of well-drawn characters, credible dialogue and a strong story. No novel should ever comment on itself, but sustain the illusion that it is enacting real events.

I met his son Martin when he was 14 – like many of us, at heart, unchanged by the decades – and in later years Kingsley always seemed proud of Martin's success. 'Great stuff,' he would say about Martin's latest novel, and I saw none of the meanness or grudging praise now credited to him.

Undoubtedly, Amis did have his mean streak, and was one of those people who feel a need to break with all their friends. His treatment of women could be crude. One of his former lovers, a student during his Swansea teaching days, told me that he would regularly order his wife into the nearby park when it was time for his 'tutorial' with her. There the novelist's wife would push the pram with the children until he drew the bedroom curtains and signalled that she could return.

17

Wise Women (1964)

Family life has always been very important to me, far more important, I suspect, than to people of my parents' generation. I often wonder why many of them bothered to have children at all, and assume that it must have been for social reasons, some ancient need to enlarge the tribe and defend the homestead, just as some people keep a dog without ever showing it affection, but feel secure when it barks at the postman.

Perhaps I belong to the first generation for whom the health and happiness of their families is a significant indicator of their own mental well-being. The family and all the emotions within it are a way of testing one's better qualities, a trampoline on which one can leap ever higher, holding one's wife and children by their hands.

I enjoyed being married, the first real security I had ever known, and easily coped with the strains and early struggles of a writer's life. I enjoyed being a father who was closely involved with his children, pushing them in their pram through the streets of Richmond and Shepperton, and later driving with them across Europe to Greece and Spain. Children change so rapidly, learning to grasp the world and learning to be happy, learning to understand themselves and shape their own minds. I was fascinated by my children and still am, and feel much the same way about my four grand-children. I have always been very proud of my children, and every moment I spend with them makes the whole of existence seem warm and meaningful.

In 1963 Mary was in good health, but needed her appendix removed. She recovered slowly from the operation at Ashford Hospital, and perhaps her resistance was affected, or some infection lingered. She was keen to go on holiday, and the following summer we drove to a rented flat at San Juan, near Alicante. For a month all went well, and we enjoyed ourselves in the bars and beach restaurants. It was the kind of holiday where the high point is the day Daddy fell off the pedalo. But Mary suddenly became ill with an infection, and this rapidly turned into severe pneumonia. Despite the local doctor, a male nurse (the practicante) who was with her constantly, and a consultant from Alicante, she died three days later. Towards the end, when she could barely breathe, she held my hand and asked: 'Am I dying?' I'm not sure if she could hear me, but I shouted that I loved her until the end. In the final seconds, when her eyes were fixed, the doctor massaged her chest, forcing the blood into her brain. Her eyes swivelled and stared at me, as if seeing me for the first time.

We buried her in the small Protestant cemetery in Alicante, a walled stone yard with a few graves of British holidaymakers killed in yachting accidents. A Protestant priest came to see me the previous day, a decent and kindly Spaniard who did not seem upset when I declined to pray with him. I can still hear the sound of the iron-wheeled cart carrying the coffin across the stony ground. The priest conducted a short service, watched by myself and the children, and a few English residents from our apartment building. Then the priest rolled up his sleeves, took a spade and began to shovel the soil onto the coffin.

In late September, when San Juan beach was deserted and the cold air was beginning to come down from the mountains, we left the now-empty apartment building and set off on the long drive back to England.

From the start I was determined to keep my family together. Mary's sisters and mother, who were an enormous help over the coming years, offered to share bringing them up. But I felt that I owed it to Mary to look after her children, and I probably needed them more than they needed me.

I did my best to be both mother and father to them, though it was extremely rare in the 1960s to find single fathers caring for their children. Many people (who should

Fay, Jim and Beatrice at home with me in 1965.

have known better) openly told me that a mother's loss was irreplaceable and the children would be affected for ever, as maintained by the child psychiatrist John Bowlby. But I seriously doubt this claim, which seems unlikely given the hazards of childbirth – the evolutionary disadvantages if the claim were true would have been selected against and a less dangerous parental bond would have taken its place. I believe that the chief threat posed by a mother's death is, rather, an uncaring or absentee father. As long as the surviving parent is loving and remains close to the children, they will thrive.

I loved my children deeply, as they knew, and we were lucky that I had a job as a writer that allowed me to be with them all the time. I made them breakfast and drove them to school, then wrote until it was time to collect them. Since day-time babysitters were difficult to come by, we did everything together – shopping, seeing friends, visiting museums, going on holiday, doing homework, watching television. In 1965 we drove to Greece for nearly two months, a wonderful holiday when we were always together. I remember a hold-up on a mountain road in the Peloponnese when an American woman looked into our car and said: 'You mean you're alone with these three?' and I replied: 'With these three you're never alone.' Thankfully, I had long forgotten what it was like to be alone.

I hope the children realised early on that they could always rely on me. My son Jim, who was the oldest, grieved deeply for his mother, but we helped each other through, and eventually he regained his confidence and became a cheerful teenager with a charming and witty sense of humour. My daughters Fay and Bea soon took command of the situation, and became strong-willed young women before they were in their teens, deciding on our diet, which holiday hotels we should stay at, what clothes they should buy. In many ways my three children brought me up.

Alcohol was a close friend and confidant in the early days; I usually had a strong Scotch and soda when I had driven the children to school and sat down to write soon after nine. In those days I finished drinking at about the time today that I start. A friendly microclimate unfurled itself from the bottle of Johnnie Walker and encouraged my imagination to emerge from its burrow and test the air. Kingsley Amis made a point of inviting me out to lunch, and in the evening I would often visit Keats Grove, where he and Elizabeth Jane Howard had rented a flat. Jane was unfailingly kind, though my presence was probably a nuisance. She cooked supper, which we ate on our knees, while Kingsley kept a beady eye on a television quiz show, answering all the questions before they were out of the compère's mouth. I am grateful to Kingsley, and glad that I saw his generous and kindly side before he became a professional curmudgeon.

Other friends were a great help, especially Michael Moorcock and his wife Hilary. But, as every bereaved person learns, one soon reaches the point where friends can do little more than keep one's glass filled. I missed Mary in a thousand and one domestic ways – the traces she had left of herself in the kitchen, bedroom and bathroom together formed the outlines of a huge void. Her absence was a space in our lives that I could almost embrace. Long months of celibacy followed, during which I resented the sight of happily married couples strolling down Shepperton High Street. I once saw a couple laughing together in the car ahead of me and sounded my horn in anger. After celibacy came a kind of desperate promiscuity, a form of shock treatment in which I was trying to will myself to come alive. I remember embracing my first lover – the estranged wife of a friend – like a survivor at sea clinging to a rescuer. I'm grateful to those friends of Mary's who rallied round and knew that it was time to bring me back into the light. In their way they were thinking of Mary rather than me, wise and kindly women who were concerned that Mary's children should be happy.

A year or so after Mary's death I saw her in a dream. She was walking past our house, skirt floating on the air, smiling cheerfully to herself. She saw me watching her from the doorstep of our house and walked on, smiling at me over her shoulder. When I woke I tried to keep these moments alive in my mind, but I knew that in her way she was saying good-bye, and that at last I was beginning to recover.

I am sure that I changed greatly during these years. On the one hand I was glad to be so close to my children. As long as they were happy nothing else mattered, and success or failure as a writer was a minor concern. At the same time I felt that nature had committed a dreadful crime against Mary and her children. Why? There was no answer to the question, which obsessed me for decades to come.

18

The Atrocity Exhibition (1966)

But perhaps there was an answer, using a kind of extreme logic. My direction as a writer changed after Mary's death, and many readers thought that I became far darker. But I like to think I was much more radical, in a desperate attempt to prove that black was white, that two and two made five in the moral arithmetic of the 1960s. I was trying to construct an imaginative logic that made sense of Mary's death and would prove that the assassination of President Kennedy and the countless deaths of the Second World War had been worthwhile or even meaningful in some as yet undiscovered way. Then, perhaps, the ghosts inside my head, the old beggar under his quilt of snow, the strangled Chinese at the railway station, Kennedy and my young wife, could be laid to rest.

All this can be seen in the pieces I began to write in the mid 1960s, which later became *The Atrocity Exhibition*. Kennedy's assassination presided over everything, an event that was sensationalised by the new medium of television.

The endless photographs of the Dealey Plaza shooting, the Zapruder film of the president dying in his wife's arms in his open-topped limousine, created a kind of gruesome overload where real sympathy began to leak away and only sensation was left, as Andy Warhol quickly realised. For me the Kennedy assassination was the catalyst that ignited the 1960s. Perhaps his death, like the sacrifice of a tribal king, would re-energise us all and bring life again to the barren meadows?

The 1960s were a far more revolutionary time than younger people now realise, and most assume that English life has always been much as it is today, except for mobile phones, emails and computers. But a social revolution took place, as significant in many ways as that of the post-war Labour government. Pop music and the space age, drugs and Vietnam, fashion and consumerism merged together into an exhilarating and volatile mix.

Emotion, and emotional sympathy, drained out of everything, and the fake had its own special authenticity. I was in many ways an onlooker, bringing up my children in a quiet suburb, taking them to children's parties and chatting to the mothers outside the school gates. But I also went to a great many parties, and smoked a little pot, though I remained a whisky and soda man. In many ways the 1960s were a fulfilment of all that I hoped would happen in England. Waves of change were overtaking each other, and at times it seemed that change would become a new kind of boredom, disguising the truth that everything beneath the gaudy surface remained the same.

In 1965 I met Dr Martin Bax, a north London paediatrician who published a quarterly poetry magazine called *Ambit*. We became firm friends, and years later I learned that his wife, Judy, was the daughter of the Lunghua headmaster, the Reverend George Osborne. She and her mother had returned to England in the 1930s and spent the war years there. I began to write my more experimental stories for *Ambit*, partly in an attempt to gain publicity for the magazine. Randolph Churchill, son of Winston and a friend of the Kennedys, objected publicly to my story 'Plan for the Assassination of Jacqueline Kennedy'. Churchill made a song and dance in the newspapers, demanding that *Ambit*'s modest Arts Council grant be withdrawn and describing my piece as an irresponsible slander, all this at a time when the ordeal of Mrs Kennedy and her courtship by Aristotle Onassis were ruthlessly exploited by the tabloid newspapers, the real target of my satire.

A prime engine of change in the 1960s was the entirely casual use of drugs, a generational culture in its own right. Many of the drugs, led by cannabis and amphetamines, were recreational, but others, heroin chief among them, were intended for use in the intensive care unit and the terminal cancer ward, and were highly dangerous. Moral outrage had a field day, while preposterous claims were made for the transformation of the imagination that could be brought about by LSD. The parents' generation fought from behind a barricade of gin and tonics, while the young proclaimed alcohol to be the real enemy of promise.

Tired of all this, and feeling that the entire wrangle about drugs was ripe for a small send-up, I suggested to Martin Bax that *Ambit* should run a competition for the best poem or short story written under the influence of drugs – a reasonable suggestion, given the huge claims made for drugs by rival gurus of the underground. This time Lord Goodman, legal fixer for the Prime Minister Harold Wilson, denounced *Ambit* for committing a public mischief (a criminal offence) and in effect threatened us with prosecution. The competition was conducted seriously, and the drugs involved ranged from amphetamines to baby aspirin. It was won by the novelist Ann Quin, for a story written under the influence of the contraceptive pill.

Another of my suggestions was staged at the ICA, when we hired a stripper, Euphoria Bliss, to perform a striptease to the reading of a scientific paper. This strange event, almost impossible to take in at the time, has stayed in my mind ever since. It still seems in the true spirit of Dada, and an example of the fusion of science and pornography that *The Atrocity Exhibition* expected to take place in the near future. Many of the imaginary 'experiments' described in the book, where panels of volunteer housewives are exposed to hours of pornographic films and then tested for their responses (!), have since been staged in American research institutes.

I must say that I admire Martin Bax for never flinching whenever I suggested my latest madcap notion. He was, after all, a practising physician, and Lord Goodman may well have had friends on the General Medical Council. Martin responded positively to my wish to bring more science into the pages of *Ambit*. Most poets were products of English Literature schools, and showed it; poetry readings were a special form of social deprivation. In some rather dingy hall a sad little cult would listen to their cut-price shaman speaking in voices, feel their emotions vaguely stirred and drift away to a darkened tube station.

I wanted more science in *Ambit*, since science was reshaping the world, and less poetry. Asked what my policy was as so-called prose editor of *Ambit*, I would reply: to get rid of the poetry. After meeting Dr Christopher Evans, a psychologist who worked at the National Physical Laboratory, not far from Shepperton, I asked him to contribute to *Ambit*. We published a remarkable series of computer-generated poems, which Martin said were as good as the real thing. I went further: they were the real thing.

Chris Evans drove into my life at the wheel of a Ford Galaxy, a huge American convertible that he soon swapped for a Mini-Cooper, a high-performance car not much bigger than a bullet that travelled at about the same speed. Chris was the first 'hoodlum scientist' I had met, and he became the closest friend I have made in my life. In appearance he resembled Vaughan, the auto-destructive hero of my novel *Crash*, though he himself was nothing like that deranged figure. Most scientists in the 1960s, especially at a government laboratory, wore white lab coats over a collar and tie, squinted at the world over the rims of their glasses and were rather stooped and conventional. Glamour played no part in their job description.

Chris, by contrast, raced around his laboratory in American sneakers, jeans and a denim shirt open to reveal an Iron Cross on a gold chain, his long black hair and craggy profile giving him a handsomely Byronic air. I never met a woman who wasn't immediately under his spell. A natural actor, he was at his best on the lecture platform, and played to his audience's emotions like a matinee idol, a young Olivier with a degree in computer science. He was hugely popular on television, and presented a number of successful series, including *The Mighty Micro*. Although running a research department of his own, Chris became an ex officio publicity manager for the NPL as a whole, and probably the only scientist in that important institution known to the public at large.

In private, surprisingly, Chris was a very different man: quiet, thoughtful and even rather shy, a good listener and an excellent drinking companion. Some of the happiest hours in my life have been spent with him in the riverside pubs between Teddington and Shepperton. In many ways his extrovert persona was a costume that he put on to hide a strain of diffidence, but I think this inner modesty was what appealed to the American astronauts and senior scientists he met during the making of his television programmes. He was a great lover of America, and especially the Midwest states, and liked nothing better than flying into Phoenix or Houston, hiring a convertible and setting off on the long drive to LA or San Francisco. He liked the easy formulas of American life. He thoroughly approved of my wish to see England Americanise itself, and hung California licence plates over his desk as a first step.

After taking his PhD in psychology at Reading University, Chris specialised in computers, and spent a year at Duke University, home to Professor Rhine and the ESP experiments that involved closed rooms and volunteers guessing each other's card sequences. Chris's American wife, Nancy, a beautiful and rather remote woman, was Rhine's secretary when he met her. ESP experiments were largely discredited in the 1960s, but I think Chris still had a sneaking hope that telepathic phenomena existed on some undiscovered level of the mind. Now and then, as we hoisted our pints and threw pieces of our cheese rolls to the Shepperton swans, he would slip some reference to ESP into the conversation, waiting for my response. He was also surprisingly interested in Scientology, while claiming to be a complete sceptic. I sometimes wonder if his entire interest in psychology was unconsciously a quest for a paranormal dimension to mental life.

I often visited Chris's lab, and admired the American licence plates and the photographs of him with Aldrin and Armstrong (this was before the lunar flights in 1969). I was fascinated by the work his team was doing on visual and language perception. In the 1970s he was exploring the possibilities of computerised medical diagnosis, after the discovery that patients would be far more frank about their symptoms when talking to a computerised image of a doctor rather than the doctor himself. Women patients from ethnic minorities would never discuss gynaecological matters with a male doctor, but spoke freely to a computerised female image.

I was sitting in his office in the early 1970s when something in the waste basket beside his desk caught my eye, a handout from a pharmaceutical company about a new antidepressant. Seeing my eyes light up, Chris offered to send me the contents of his waste basket from then on. Every week a huge envelope arrived, packed with handouts, brochures, research papers and annual reports from university labs and psychiatric institutions, a cornucopia of fascinating material that fired my imagination. Eventually I stored them in an old coal bunker outside the kitchen door. Twenty years later, when I dismantled the bunker, I started reading these ancient handouts as I rested between axe blows. They were as fascinating and stimulating as they had been when I first read them.

Chris's death from cancer in 1979 was a tragic loss to his family and friends, all of whom have vivid memories of him.

In 1964 Michael Moorcock took over the editorship of the leading British science fiction magazine, *New Worlds*, determined to change it in every way he could. For years we had carried on noisy but friendly arguments about the right direction for science fiction to take. American and Russian astronauts were carrying out regular orbital flights in their spacecraft, and everyone assumed that NASA would land an American on the moon in 1969 and fulfil President Kennedy's vow on coming to office. Communications satellites had transformed the media landscape of the planet, bringing the Vietnam War live into every living room.

Surprisingly, though, science fiction had failed to prosper. Most of the American magazines had closed, and the sales of *New Worlds* were a fraction of what they had been in the 1950s. I believed that science fiction had run its course, and would soon either die or mutate into outright fantasy. I flew the flag for what I termed 'inner space', in effect the psychological space apparent in surrealist painting, the short stories of Kafka, noir films at their most intense, and the strange, almost mentalised world of science labs and research institutes where Chris Evans had thrived, and which formed the setting for part of *The Atrocity Exhibition*.

Moorcock approved of my general aims, but wanted to go further. He knew that I responded strongly to 1960s London, its psychedelia, bizarre publishing ventures, the breaking-down of barriers by a new generation of artists and photo-graphers, the use of fashion as a political weapon, the youth cults and drug culture. But I was 35 and bringing up three children in the suburbs. He knew that however much I enjoyed his parties, I had to drive home and pay the baby-sitter. He was ten years younger than me, the resident guru of Ladbroke Grove and an important figure and inspiration on the music scene. It was all this counter-cultural energy that he wanted to channel into *New Worlds*. He knew that an unrestricted diet of psychedelic illustrations and typography would soon become tiring, and responded to my suggestion that he dim the LSD strobe lights a little and think in terms of British artists such as Richard Hamilton and Eduardo Paolozzi.

I still remembered the 1956 exhibition at the Whitechapel Gallery, This is Tomorrow, and I regularly visited the ICA in Dover Street. Many of its shows were put on by a small group of architects and artists, among them Hamilton and Paolozzi, who formed a kind of ideas laboratory, teasing out the visual connections between Egyptian architecture and modern refrigerator design, between Tintoretto 'crane-shots' and the swooping camera angles of Hollywood blockbusters.

In Eduardo Paolozzi's Chelsea studio, 1968.

All this was closer to science fiction, in my eyes, than the tired images of spacecraft and planetary landscapes in s-f magazines.

I remembered that in the 1950s Paolozzi had remarked in an interview that the s-f magazines published in the suburbs of Los Angeles contained more genuine imagination than anything hung on the walls of the Royal Academy (still in its Munnings phase). With Moorcock's approval, I contacted Paolozzi, whose studio was in Chelsea, and he invited us to visit him.

We got on famously from the start. In many ways Paolozzi was an intimidating figure, a thuggish man with a sculptor's huge arms and hands, a strong voice and assertive manner.

But his mind was light and flexible, he was a good listener and adept conversationalist with a keen and well-stocked mind. Original ideas tripped off his tongue, whatever the subject, and he was always pushing at the edges of some notion that intrigued him, exploring its possibilities before filing it away. A woman-friend I introduced to him exclaimed: 'He's a minotaur!' but he was a minotaur who was a judo expert and light on his feet.

He and I became firm friends for the next thirty years, and I regularly visited his studio in Dovehouse Street. I think we felt at ease with each other because we were both, in our different ways, recent immigrants to England. Paolozzi's Italian parents had settled in Edinburgh before the war, where they ran an ice cream business. After art school he left Scotland and attended the Slade in London, quickly established himself with his first one-man show, and then left for Paris for two years, meeting Giacometti, Tristan Tzara and the surrealists. He always insisted that he was a European and not a British artist. My impression is that as an art student he had felt deeply frustrated by the limitations of the London art establishment, though by the time I knew him he was well on the way to becoming one of the tallest pillars in that establishment.

Everyone who knew him will agree that Eduardo was a warm and generous personality, but at the same time remarkably quick to pick a quarrel. Perhaps this touchiness drew on the deep personal slights he suffered as an Italian boy in wartime Edinburgh, but he fell out with almost all his close friends, a trait he shared with Kingsley Amis. One of his disconcerting habits was to give his friends valuable presents of pieces of sculpture or sets of screen-prints and then, after some largely imagined slight, demand the presents back. He fell out spectacularly with the Smithsons, his close friends and collaborators on This is Tomorrow. After giving them one of his great Frog sculptures, he later informed them that he wanted it returned; when they refused, he went round to their house at night and tried to dig it out of their garden. Their friendship, needless to say, never recovered.

I have often wondered why Eduardo and I never fell out, though my partner Claire Walsh, who was present at the time, claims that we had our 'break-up' row on the second day we met. I think Eduardo realised that I was a genuine admirer of his work, and that apart from his lively imagination and powerful mind I wanted nothing from him. He was a generous and sociable man, and tended to attract an entourage of graduate students, museum curators, art school administrators eager for him to judge their diploma shows, well-to-do art lovers and ladies who lunch – in short, what used to be called sycophants. This became a real problem for him in the 1980s once he accepted his knighthood.

To what extent did Eduardo's very busy social life influence his work, possibly for the worse? I greatly admire his early sculpture, those gaunt and eroded figures cast from machine parts who resemble the survivors of a nuclear war.

It's difficult to imagine the Paolozzi of the 1980s, who dined most evenings at the Caprice, a few steps from the Ritz, producing those haunted and traumatised images of mankind at its most desperate. By the end of the 1960s his sculpture had become smooth and streamlined, and resembled modules from some high-tech design office working on a new airport terminal.

I think he was aware of this, and sometimes he would say: 'Right, Jim … let's go out.' And we would prowl the side streets off the King's Road, where he would search the builders' skips, his huge hands feeling some piece of discarded wood or metalwork, as if looking for a lost toy. Then it would be back to the Caprice, with its showbiz and film-star clientele, its dreadful acoustics and cries of 'Eduardo…!' and 'Francis…!' Why Bacon spent any time there is another mystery. Eventually, by the late 1980s, I had to retreat gently from this competitive circus.

But for the most part Eduardo enjoyed an idyllic life, and I watched him with real envy as he worked in his studio, listening to music while he cut up images for his screen-prints, chatting to an attractive graduate student, recounting another traveller's tale about his latest trip to Japan, a country that fascinated him even more than the US. His early obsession with all things American rather faded after his teaching trip to Berkeley in the late 1960s. He told me how he had taken a party of his students on a field trip to a Douglas aircraft plant, but they had been bored by the whole venture. Advanced technology might spur the imagination of a European, but Americans took it for granted, and were no more inspired by the assembly of a four-engine jet plane than by the process of sealing beans into a can.

Japan, I think, became for Eduardo the continuation of America by other means, and the excitement of an endlessly self-renewing technology lay at the centre of the Japanese dream. He would return from Japan loaded with high-tech toys, bizarre robots equipped with electronic sensors that could lumberingly make their way around his studio. He once rang me from Tokyo, and I could barely hear him above a background babble of Japanese voices. He explained that he was near a bank of cigarette automats with voice-actuated brand selectors. He shouted above the din: 'It's midnight, there's no one here. The machines break down and start each other talking...' I wish Eduardo had pursued all this in his sculpture, and can still hear the robots jabbering in the darkness, with their 'Please come again' and 'Thank you for your custom' going on through the night.

Germany was another great magnet for him, and the country where his sculpture was most admired. I remember telling him that Chris Evans had found some wartime film cans stored in a basement at the National Physical Laboratory, among them a Waffen SS instructional film on how to build a pontoon bridge. Eduardo was deeply impressed. 'That says it all,' he murmured, his imagination stirred by the fusion of these almost emblematic elite troops with the down-to-earth realities of military engineering. I suspect his obsession with Wittgenstein, the Austrian-born philosopher and Cambridge friend of Bertrand Russell, had far less to do with *The Tractatus* than with Wittgenstein's trips to the cinema to see Betty Grable.

Eduardo knew few novelists, if any, though the same could be said of myself. I felt far more at ease with a physician like Martin Bax, or with Chris Evans and Eduardo, than I did with my fellow novelists in the late 1960s. Most of them were still locked into a literary sensibility that would have been out of date in the 1920s. I'm glad to say that the novel has changed very much for the better in recent years, and a new generation of writers has emerged, among them Will Self, Martin Amis and Iain Sinclair, with powerful imaginations and a wide, roving intelligence.

The last literary party I attended, at my publishers Jonathan Cape in the early 1970s, at least brought me a little closer to the threatening Lord Goodman. I arrived with my agent, John Wolfers, a highly cultivated man who had served in the Welsh Guards and been wounded in the battle for Monte Cassino. He was also a compulsive drinker, locked into an intensely competitive relationship with the head of Cape, Tom Maschler, with whom he had been to school. The evening of the party John was deeply drunk, and barely able to stand upright. I tried to support him, but he pushed me away, talked incoherently for ten seconds and suddenly crashed to the floor, like a giant tree falling in a forest, taking two or three smaller guests with him. This happened several times, and was soon clearing the room.

Eventually I managed to steer him down the stairs. There were no taxis cruising Bedford Square, but a uniformed chauffeur stood by a double-parked limousine. Taking out a £5 note (then probably worth £50) I offered it to the chauffeur if he would take John home. 'Regent Square, five minutes away.' He accepted the fiver, and we laid John out in the rear seat. As the chauffeur started the engine I asked: 'By the way, whose car is this?' He replied: 'Lord Goodman's.'

I'm surprised I didn't find myself in the Tower.

19

Healing Times (1967)

I still think that my children brought me up, perhaps as an incidental activity to rearing themselves. We emerged from their childhood together, they as happy and confident teenagers, and I into a kind of second adulthood enriched by the experience of watching them grow from infancy into fully formed human beings with minds and ambitions of their own. Few fathers observe this extraordinary process, the most significant in all nature, and sadly a great many mothers are so distracted by the effort of running a home and family that they are scarcely aware of the countless miracles of life that take place around them every day. I think of myself as extremely lucky. The years I spent as the parent of my young children were the richest and happiest I have ever known, and I am sure that my parents' lives were arid by contrast. For them, domestic life was little more than a social annexe to the serious business of playing bridge and flirting at the Country Club.

My friendships with Eduardo Paolozzi, Dr Martin Bax,

Chris Evans and Michael Moorcock were important to me but lay on the perimeter of my life, and anyway depended on reliable babysitters and the parking regulations of the day. My children were at the centre of my life, circled at a distance by my writing. I kept up a steady output of novels and short-story collections, largely because I spent most of my time at home. A short story, or a chapter of a novel, would be written in the time between ironing a school tie, serving up the sausage and mash, and watching *Blue Peter*. I am certain that my fiction is all the better for that. My greatest ally was the pram in the hall.

The 1960s were an exciting decade that I watched on television. Driving the children to and from school, to parties and friends, I had to be very careful how much I drank, regardless of the breathalyser. I was a passive smoker of a good deal of cannabis, and once took LSD, completely unaware of the strength of a single dose. This was a disastrous blunder that opened a vent of hell, and confirmed me as a long-standing whisky drinker.

Fay and Bea had taken charge of family life, and Jim and I were happy to follow orders. This was excellent training for all of us, especially the girls. They made the most of school and university, and have enjoyed successful careers in the arts and the BBC. They married happily and have families of their own. From the start I drummed into them that they were as entitled to opportunity and success as any man, and should never allow themselves to be patronised or exploited.

My daughter Fay Ballard.

As it happened, I could have saved my breath; they knew exactly what they wanted to do with their lives, and were determined to do it.

Some fathers make good mothers, and I hope I was one of them, though most of the women who know me would say that I made a very slatternly mother, notably unkeen on housework, unaware that homes need to be cleaned now and then, and too often to be found with a cigarette in one hand and a drink in the other – in short, the kind of mother, no doubt loving and easy-going, of whom the social services deeply disapprove. The women journalists who have interviewed me over the years always refer to the dust that their gimlet eyes detect in unfrequented corners of my house. I suspect that the sight of a man bringing up apparently happy children (to which they never refer) alerts a reflex of rather old-fashioned alarm. If women aren't needed to do the dusting, what hope is there left? Perhaps, too, the compulsive cleaning of a family home is an attempt to erase those repressed emotions that threaten to break through into the daylight. The nuclear family, dominated by an over-worked mother, is in many ways deeply unnatural, as is marriage itself, part of the huge price we pay to control the male sex.

The absence of a mother was a deep loss for my children, but at least my girls were spared the stress that I noticed between many mothers and their daughters as puberty approached. As a father who collected his children from school, I spent a great deal of time by the school gates, and soon recognised the fierce maternal tension that made ado-lescence a hell for many of my daughters' friends. Some mothers simply could not cope with the growing evidence that their daughters were younger, more womanly and more sexually attractive than they were. Sex, I'm glad to say, never worried me; I was far more concerned about what might happen to my daughters in a car rather than in a bed. A few words of friendly advice and the address of the nearest family planning clinic were enough; nature and their innate good sense would do the rest.

Sadly, many mothers refused to accept that their daugh-

My daughter Beatrice Ballard.

ters had reached puberty at all. I once collected my daughters from a schoolfriend's party, the first any of them had attended where boys would be present. Mothers were chatting near their cars, waiting for the party to end, and one of them laughingly described the pitch-black living room, thudding with music, where slumped forms of their precious daughters and the boy guests sprawled on sofas. Then one of the mothers emerged from the house and gestured helplessly at her friends. She was clearly distraught, barely able to walk or speak, and tottered down the garden path towards us. 'Helen...' someone called, taking her quivering shoulders. 'Is Sally with a boy?'

Helen stared at us, as if she had seen the horror of all horrors. At last she spoke: 'She's holding his penis...'

The most important person I met in the late 1960s was Claire Walsh, who has been my partner, inspiration and life-companion for forty years. We met at a Michael Moorcock party, when Claire was in her early twenties, and I was struck immediately by her beauty and high intelligence. I often think that I have been extremely lucky during my life to have known closely four beautiful and interesting women – Mary, my daughters, and Claire. Claire is passionate, principled, argumentative and highly loyal, both to me and to her many friends. She has a wide-ranging mind, utterly free of cant, and has been very generous to my children and grand-children.

Life with Claire has always been interesting – we have often driven together across half of Europe and never once stopped talking. We share a huge number of interests, in painting and architecture, wine, foreign travel, politics (she is keenly left-wing and impatient with my middle-of-the-roadism), the cinema and, most important of all, good food. For many years we have eaten out twice a week, and Claire is an expert judge of restaurants, frequently finding a superb new place long before the critics discover it. She is a great reader of newspapers and magazines, has completely mastered the internet and is always supplying me with news stories that she knows will appeal to me. She is a great cook, and over the years has educated my palate. She has very gamely put up with my lack of interest in music and the theatre. Above all, she has been a staunch supporter of my writing, and the best friend that I have had.

When I first met Claire I was dazzled by her great beauty, naturally blonde hair and elegant profile. Sadly, she has suffered more than her share of ill health. Soon after we met, she underwent a major kidney operation at a London hospital, and I remember walking with her down the Charing Cross Road on the day she was discharged, on the way to Foyle's to buy the 'book' of her operation, a medical text of the exact surgical procedure. It is typical of Claire that she took the trouble to write a letter of thanks to the surgeon who invented the procedure, then retired to New Zealand, and received a long and interesting reply from him. Ten years ago she faced the challenge of breast cancer, but fought back bravely, an ordeal that lasted many years. That she triumphed is a tribute to her courage.

Together we have travelled all over Europe and America, to film festivals and premieres, where she has looked after me and kept up my spirits. At the time we met, Claire was working as the publicity manager for a publisher of art books, and she went onto be publicity manager of Gollancz, Michael Joseph and Allen Lane. Her knowledge of publishing, and many of the devious and likeable personalities involved, has been invaluable.

Looking back, I realise that there is scarcely a city, museum or beach in Europe that I don't associate with Claire. We have spent thousands of the happiest hours with our children (she has a daughter Jennifer) on beaches and under poolside umbrellas, in hotels and restaurants, walking around cathedrals from Chartres to Rome and Seville. Claire is a speed-reader of guidebooks, and always finds some interesting side chapel, or points out the special symbolism of this or that saint in a Van Eyck. She had a Catholic upbringing, and lived in a flat not far from Westminster Cathedral, whose nave was virtually her childhood playground. Whenever we find ourselves in Victoria she casually points out a stone lion or Peabody building where she and her friends played hide-and-seek.

I was so impressed by Claire's beauty that I made her the centrepiece of two of my 'advertisements', which were published in *Ambit*, *Ark* and elsewhere in the late 1960s. I was advertising abstract notions largely taken from *The Atrocity Exhibition*, such as 'Does the Angle Between Two Walls Have a Happy Ending?' – a curious question that for some reason preoccupied me at the time. In each of the full-page ads the text was superimposed on a glossy, high-quality photograph, and the intention was to take paid advertisement pages in *Vogue* and *Harper's Bazaar*. I reasoned that most novels could dispense with almost all their text and reduce themselves to a single evocative slogan. I outlined my proposal in an application to the Arts Council, but they rather solemnly

Claire Walsh in 1968.

refused to award me a grant, on the surprising grounds that my application was frivolous. This disappointed me, as I was completely serious, and the Arts Council awarded tens of thousands of pounds to fund activities that, unconsciously or not, were clearly jokes – *Ambit* itself could fall into that category, along with the *London Magazine*, the *New Review* and countless poetry magazines and little presses.

The funds disbursed by the Arts Council over the decades have created a dependent client class of poets, novelists and weekend publishers whose chief mission in life is to get their grants renewed, as anyone attending a poetry magazine's parties will quickly learn from the nearby conversations. Why the taxes of people on modest incomes (the source of most taxes today) should pay for the agreeable hobby of a north London children's doctor, or a self-important Soho idler like the late editor of the *New Review*, is something I have never understood. I assume that the patronage of the arts by the state serves a political role by performing a castration ceremony, neutering any revolutionary impulse and reducing the 'arts community' to a docile herd. They are allowed to bleat, but are too enfeebled to ever paw the ground.

Still, what the Arts Council saw as a prank at least put Claire's beautiful face into the *Evening Standard*.

And, last but not least, she introduced me to the magic of cats.

20

New Sculpture (1969)

If *The Atrocity Ehibition* was a firework display in a charnel house, *Crash* was a thousand-bomber raid on reality, though English critics at the time thought that I had lost my bearings and made myself into the most vulnerable target. *The Atrocity Exhibition* was published in 1970, and was my attempt to make sense of the sixties, a decade when so much seemed to change for the better. Hope, youth and freedom were more than slogans; for the first time since 1939 people were no longer fearful of the future. The print-dominated past had given way to an electronic present, a realm where instantaneity ruled.

At the same time, darker currents were flowing a little too close to the surface. The viciousness of the Vietnam War, lingering public guilt over the Kennedy assassination, the casualties of the hard drug scene, the determined effort by the entertainment culture to infantilise us – all these had begun to get between us and the new dawn. Youth began to seem rather old hat and, anyway, what could we do with all that hope and freedom? Instantaneity allowed too many things to happen at once. Sexual fantasies fused with science, politics and celebrity while truth and reason were shouldered towards the door. We watched the *Mondo Cane* 'documentaries' where it was impossible to tell the fake newsreel footage of atrocities and executions from the real.

And we rather liked it that way. Our willing complicity in this blurring of truth and reality in the *Mondo Cane* films alone made them possible, and was taken up by the entire media landscape, by politicians and churchmen. Celebrity was all that counted. If denying God made a bishop famous, what choice was there? We liked mood music, promises that were never kept, slogans that were meaningless. Our darkest fantasies were pushing at a half-open bathroom door as Marilyn Monroe lay drugged among the fading bubbles.

All this I tried to grapple with in *The Atrocity Exhibition*. What if the everyday environment was itself a huge mental breakdown: how could we know if we were sane or psychotic? Were there any rituals we could perform, deranged sacraments assembled from a kit of desperate fears and phobias, that would conjure up a more meaningful world?

Writing *The Atrocity Exhibition*, I adopted an approach as fragmented as the world it described. Most readers found it difficult to grasp, expecting a conventional A+B+C narrative, and were put off by the isolated paragraphs and the rather obsessive sexual fantasies about the prominent figures of the day. But the book has remained in print in Britain,

Europe and the USA, and has been reissued many times.

In New York it was published by Doubleday, but the editor, an enthusiastic supporter, made the mistake of adding an advance copy to the trolley filled with new titles that was sent up to the president's office. There Nelson Doubleday broke the cardinal rule of all American publishers: never read one of your own books. He leafed idly through *The Atrocity Exhibition* and his eye lit upon a piece entitled 'Why I Want to Fuck Ronald Reagan'. The then governor of California was a close friend, and within minutes the order had gone out to pulp the entire edition. The book was later published by Grove Press, home to William Burroughs and other prominent avant-garde writers, and since the 1990s by the very lively and adventurous Re/Search firm in San Francisco, one of the most remarkable publishing houses I have come across, specialists in urban anthropology of the most bizarre kind.

In the last few years *The Atrocity Exhibition* seems to be emerging from the dark, and I wonder if the widespread use of the internet has made my experimental novel a great deal more accessible. The short paragraphs and discontinuities of the morning's emails, the overlapping texts and the need to switch one's focus between unrelated topics, together create a fragmentary world very like the text of *The Atrocity Exhibition*.

*   *   *

By the time that *The Atrocity Exhibition* was published in 1970 I was already looking ahead to what would be my first 'conventional' novel for five years. I thought hard about the cluster of ideas that later made up *Crash*, many of them explored in *The Atrocity Exhibition*, where to some extent they were disguised within the fragmentary narrative. *Crash* would be a head-on charge into the arena, an open attack on all the conventional assumptions about our dislike of violence in general and sexual violence in particular. Human beings, I was sure, had far darker imaginations than we liked to believe. We were ruled by reason and self-interest, but only when it suited us to be rational, and much of the time we chose to be entertained by films, novels and comic strips that deployed horrific levels of cruelty and violence.

In *Crash* I would openly propose a strong connection between sexuality and the car crash, a fusion largely driven by the cult of celebrity. It seemed obvious that the deaths of famous people in car crashes resonated far more deeply than their deaths in plane crashes or hotel fires, as one could see from Kennedy's death in his Dallas motorcade (a special kind of car crash), to the grim and ghastly death of Princess Diana in the Paris underpass.

Crash would clearly be a challenge, and I was still not completely convinced by my deviant thesis. Then in 1970 someone at the New Arts Laboratory in London contacted me and asked if there was anything I would like to do there. The large building, a disused pharmaceutical warehouse, contained a theatre, a cinema and an art gallery (there were also a number of flues, intended to draw off any dangerous chemical fumes and useful, so I was told, for venting away any cannabis smoke in the event of a police raid.

It occurred to me that I could test my hypothesis about the unconscious links between sex and the car crash by putting on an exhibition of crashed cars. The Arts Lab were keen to help, and offered me the gallery for a month. I drove around various wrecked-car sites in north London, and paid for three cars, including a crashed Pontiac, to be delivered to the gallery.

The cars went on show without any supporting graphic material, as if they were large pieces of sculpture. A TV enthusiast at the Arts Lab offered to set up a camera and closed-circuit monitors on which the guests could watch themselves as they strolled around the crashed cars. I agreed, and suggested that we hire a young woman to interview the guests about their reactions. Contacted by telephone, she agreed to appear naked, but when she walked into the gallery and saw the crashed cars she told me that she would only perform topless, a significant response in its own right, I felt at the time.

I ordered a fair quantity of alcohol, and treated the first night like any gallery opening, having invited a cross section of writers and journalists. I have never seen the guests at an art gallery get drunk so quickly. There was a huge tension in the air, as if everyone felt threatened by some inner alarm that had started to ring. No one would have noticed the cars if they had been parked in the street outside, but under the unvarying gallery lights these damaged vehicles seemed to provoke and disturb. Wine was splashed over the cars, windows were broken, and the topless girl was almost raped in the back seat of the Pontiac (or so she claimed: she later wrote a damning review headed 'Ballard Crashes' in the underground paper *Friendz*). A woman journalist from *New Society* began to interview me among the mayhem, but became so overwrought with indignation, of which the journal had an unlimited supply, that she had to be restrained from attacking me.

During the month they were on show the cars were ceaselessly attacked, daubed with white paint by a Hare Krishna group, overturned and stripped of wing mirrors and licence plates. By the time the show closed and the cars were towed away, unmourned the moment they were dragged through the gallery doors, I had long since made up my mind. All my suspicions had been confirmed about the unconscious links that my novel would explore. My exhibition had in fact been a psychological test disguised as an art show, which is probably true of Hirst's shark and Emin's bed. I suspect that it's no longer possible to stir or outrage spectators by aesthetic means alone, as did the Impressionists and cubists. A psychological challenge is needed that threatens one of our dearer delusions, whether a stained sheet or a bisected cow forced to endure a second death in order to remind us of the illusions to which we cling about the first.

In 1970, encouraged by my crashed cars exhibition, I began to write *Crash*. This was more than a literary challenge, not least because I had three young children crossing the streets of Shepperton every day, and nature might have played another of its nasty tricks. I have described the novel as a kind of psychopathic hymn, and it took an immense effort of will to enter the minds of the central characters. In an attempt to be faithful to my own imagination, I gave the narrator my own name, accepting all that this entailed.

Two weeks after finishing the novel I was involved in a car crash of my own, when my tank-like Ford Zephyr had a front-wheel blowout at the foot of Chiswick Bridge. The car swerved out of control, crossed the central reservation and rolled onto its back. Luckily I was wearing my seat belt. Hanging upside down, I found that the doors had been jammed by the partly collapsed roof. People were shouting: 'Petrol! Petrol!' The car lay in the centre of the oncoming carriageway, and I was fortunate not to be struck by the approaching traffic. Eventually I wound down the window and clambered out. An ambulance took me to a nearby hospital at Roehampton, where my head was X-rayed. I had mild concussion for a fortnight, a constant headache that suddenly cleared, and was otherwise unhurt.

Looking back, I suspect that if I had died the accident might well have been judged deliberate, at least on the unconscious level, a surrender to the dark powers that propelled the novel. I have never had an accident since, and in half a century of driving have never made an insurance claim. But I believe that *Crash* is less a hymn to death than an attempt to appease death, to buy off the executioner who waits for us all in a quiet garden nearby, like Bacon's headless figure in his herringbone jacket who sits patiently at a table with a machine gun beside him. *Crash* is set at a point where sex and death intersect, though the graph is difficult to read and is constantly recalibrating itself. The same is true, I suppose, of Tracey Emin's bed, which reminds us that this young woman's beautiful body has stepped from a dishevelled grave.

Crash has been published in many countries, and was widely reissued after the 1996 David Cronenberg film. It was a moderate success in Britain, but Jonathan Cape showed none of the flair of their French counterparts, Calman-Levy in Paris. The French edition was a huge success, and remains my best-known book in France. The French critics accepted without qualms the novel's yoking together of sex, death and the motor car. Anyone who drives in France is steering into the pages of *Crash*.

An important factor in the French success of *Crash* was

the long tradition of subversive works in France, going back at least as far as the pornographic novels of de Sade and extending more recently from the symbolist poets to the anti-clerical fantasies of the surrealists and the novels of Céline and Genet. No such tradition has ever existed in England, and it is impossible to imagine *Story of O* being published here in the 1950s. The United States, now fast becoming a theocratic state run by right-wing political fanatics and religious moralisers, has posed similar problems to its more challenging writers. Nabokov's *Lolita*, Henry Miller's *Tropic* novels, and William Burroughs' *Naked Lunch* were all first published in Paris by the Olympia Press, a small publishing house that specialised in literary porn.

Crash created little stir when it first appeared in Britain, but twenty-five years later, after a period when the country was supposed to have liberalised itself, a preposterous storm in the largest teacup that Fleet Street could find showed just how repressed and silly as a nation we could be.

David Cronenberg's film of *Crash* was premiered at the Cannes Film Festival in 1996. It was the most controversial film of the festival, and the controversy continued for years afterwards, especially in England. Desperate Conservative politicians, facing defeat at the imminent general election, attacked the film in an attempt to gain moral credit as the guardians of public decency. One cabinet minister, Virginia Bottomley, called for the film (which she had not seen) to be banned.

The Cannes festival is an extraordinary media event, in many ways deeply intimidating to a mere novelist. Books may still be read in vast numbers, but films are dreamed. Claire and I were stunned by the screaming crowds, the lavish parties and stretch limos. I took part in all the publicity interviews, and was deeply impressed to see how committed the stars of the film were to Cronenberg's elegant adaptation of my novel.

I was sitting next to Holly Hunter when we were joined by a leading American film critic. His first question was: 'Holly, what are you doing in this shit?' Holly sprang into life, and delivered a passionate defence of the film, castigating him for his small-mindedness and provincialism. It was the greatest performance of the festival, which I cheered vigorously.

The film opened in France within a few weeks, and was very successful, and then went on to open across Europe and the rest of the world. In America there were problems when Ted Turner, who controlled the distribution company, decided that *Crash* might offend public decency. At the time, interestingly, he was married to Jane Fonda, who had enlivened her career by playing prostitutes (as in *Klute*) or cavorting naked in a fur-lined spaceship (in *Barbarella*).

In England the film was delayed for a year when Westminster Council banned it from the West End of London, and a number of other councils up and down the country followed suit. When the film finally opened there were no copycat car crashes, and the controversy at last died down. Cronenberg, a highly intelligent and thoughtful man, was completely baffled by the English reaction. 'Why?' he kept asking me. 'What's going on here?'

After fifty years, I was nowhere nearer an answer.

21

Lunches and Films (1987)

By 1980 my three children were adults and away at their universities. Within a year or two they would leave home and begin their careers apart from me, and the richest and most fulfilling period in my life would abruptly come to an end. I had already had a foretaste of this. As every parent knows, infancy and childhood seem to last for ever. Then adolescence arrives and promptly leaves on the next bus, and one is sharing the family home with likeable young adults who are more intelligent, better company and in many ways wiser than oneself. But childhood has gone, and in the silence one stares at the empty whisky bottles in the pantry and wonders if any number of drinks will fill the void.

We had enjoyed the 1970s together, the dull Heath years and the twilight world of the last Old Labour government, largely by going abroad whenever we could. Claire and I and our four children would climb into my large family saloon and head for Dover, watch the white cliffs recede without a pang (I never saw a tear shed by a single fellow passenger on

247

countless cross-channel ferries) and begin to breathe freely as we emerged through the bow doors and rolled the wheels across the Boulogne cobbles. Soon there was the intoxicating reek of Gauloises, scent, merde and higher octane French petrol – now sadly all gone, including the cobbles. For reasons I have never understood, we took few photographs, and had left it too late when the children decided to holiday on their own. But memory is the greatest gallery in the world, and I can play an endless archive of images of the happy time.

Waving goodbye to the children as Claire and I set off on our first holiday alone, I found myself thinking of Shanghai again. I had almost forgotten the war, and never referred to Shanghai in conversation with friends, and rarely even to Claire and the children. But I had always wanted to write about the war years and internment, partly because so few people in England were aware of the Pacific war against the Japanese.

It was then nearly forty years since I entered Lunghua Camp, and soon my memories would fade. Few novelists have waited so long to write about the most formative experiences of their lives, and I am still puzzled why I allowed so many decades to slip by. Perhaps, as I have often reflected, it took me twenty years to forget Shanghai and twenty years to remember. During my early years in England after the war Shanghai had become an unattainable city, an El Dorado buried beneath a past to which I could never return. Another reason was that I was waiting for my children to grow up.

Until they were young adults I was too protective of them to expose them in my mind to the dangers I had known at their age.

One question that readers still ask is: why did you leave your parents out of the novel? When I first began to think about the overall story I assumed that the central characters would be adults, and that children of any age would play no part in the novel. But I realised that I had no adult memories of Lunghua Camp, or of Shanghai. My only memories of life in both the camp and the city were those of an early teenager. I had, and still have, vivid memories of cycling around Shanghai, exploring empty apartment buildings, and trying unsuccessfully to fraternise with Japanese soldiers. But I had no memories of going to nightclubs and dinner parties. Although I spent my time roaming around Lunghua Camp, I had little idea of large areas of adult life. To this day I know nothing about the sexual lives of the internees. Did they have affairs, in the warrens of curtained cubicles that must have been ideal trysting cells? Almost certainly, I assume, especially during the first year when the internees' health was still robust. Were there pregnancies? Yes, and the few families involved were moved by the Japanese to camps in Shanghai that were close to hospitals. Were there fierce rivalries and gnawing tensions between the internees? Yes, and I observed rows and arguments between both men and women that sometimes came to blows. But I knew nothing about the festering resentments that must have lasted for months if not years. My father was a gregarious man and got on well with most people, but my mother made few friends in G Block and seemed to spend most of her time reading in our little room. Curiously, though we ate, slept, dressed and undressed within a few feet of each other, I have very few memories of her in the camp. And none of my sister.

So, I accepted what I had probably assumed from the start, that *Empire of the Sun* would be seen through the eyes of a child who became a teenager during war and internment. And there seemed no point in inventing a fictitious child when I had one ready-made to hand: my younger self. Once I decided that the novel would be autobiographical, everything fell naturally into place. In much of the novel I was describing events I could still see in my mind's eye. There were a huge number of memories that I needed to knit together, and some of the events described are imaginary, but although *Empire of the Sun* is a novel it is firmly based on true experiences, either my own or those told to me by other internees.

Writing the novel was surprisingly painless. A rush of memories rose from my typescript, the filth and cruelty of Shanghai, the faded smell of deserted villages, even the stench of Lunghua Camp, the reek of overcrowded barrack huts and dormitories, the desperate seediness of what in effect was a large slum. I was frisking myself of memories that popped out of every pocket. By the time I finished, at the end of 1983, Shanghai had advanced out of its own mirage and become a real city again

Empire of the Sun was a huge success, the only one I have known on that scale, and outsold all my previous books put together. It revived my backlist, in Britain and abroad, and drew many new readers to my earlier books. Some were deeply disappointed, writing letters along the lines of 'Mr Ballard, could you explain what you really mean by your novel *Crash*?' A question with no possible answer.

Other, more sympathetic readers of my earlier novels and short stories were quick to spot echoes of *Empire of the Sun*. The trademark images that I had set out over the previous thirty years – the drained swimming pools, abandoned hotels and nightclubs, deserted runways and flooded rivers – could all be traced back to wartime Shanghai. For a long time I resisted this, but I accept now that it is almost certainly true. The memories of Shanghai that I had tried to repress had been knocking at the floorboards under my feet, and had slipped quietly into my fiction. At the same time, though, I have always been fascinated by deserts, and even wrote an entire book, *Vermilion Sands*, set at a desert resort something like Palm Springs. And yet there are no deserts within a thousand miles of Shanghai, and the only sand I ever saw was in the snake house at Shanghai Zoo.

*   *   *

Most writers dream of having films made of their novels, but for every thousand films visualised and enthused over during the world's longest lunches only one is ever actually made. The film world is a gaudy balloon kept aloft by enthusiasm, preposterous overconfidence, and all the dreams that money can buy. Film people – producers, directors and actors – are enormously good company, far livelier and more interesting than the majority of writers, and without their enthusiasm and their heroic lunches few films would ever reach the screen.

I was lucky enough to have options taken out on my earlier novels, but unlucky that my career as a writer coincided with the decades which marked the decline of the British film industry. Films based on my novels were lunched, but never launched.

The first time I saw my name (even if mispelled) in the credits of a film came in 1970, with the British release of *When Dinosaurs Ruled the Earth*. This was a Hammer film, a sequel to the Raquel Welch vehicle *One Million Years BC*, itself a remake of the 1940 Hollywood original starring Victor Mature and Carole Landis. Hammer specialised in Dracula and Frankenstein films, then much despised by the critics. But their films had tremendous panache and visual attack, without a single wasted frame, and the directors were surprisingly free to push their obsessions to the limit.

I was contacted by a Hammer producer, Aida Young, who was a great admirer of *The Drowned World*. She was keen that I write the screenplay for their next production, a sequel to *One Million Years BC*. Curious to see how the British film world worked, I turned up at the Wardour Street offices of Hammer, to be greeted in the foyer by a huge Tyrannosaurus rex about to deflower a blonde-haired actress in a leopard-skin bikini. The credits screamed 'Curse of the Dinosaurs!'

Had the film already been made? I knew that outfits like Hammer worked fast. But Aida assured me that this was just window dressing, and they had settled on the title *When Dinosaurs Ruled the Earth*. Raquel Welch would not be available. They were thinking of using a Czech actress who spoke no English, but this didn't matter since there would be no dialogue in the film. My job was to come up with a strong story.

She steered me into the office of Tony Hinds, then the head of Hammer. He was affable but gloomy, and listened without comment as Aida launched into a chapter-by-chapter account of *The Drowned World*, with its picture of a steaming, half-submerged London and its vistas of dream-inducing water.

She finished and we waited for Hinds to speak. 'Water?' he repeated. 'We've had a lot of trouble with water.'

It turned out that they planned to shoot the film in the Canary Islands. I remembered that the surrealists had made field trips to the Canaries, fascinated by the black volcanic beaches and the extraordinary fauna and flora. All Hammer had seen was the tax incentives.

Hinds asked me what ideas I had come up with. Bearing in mind that the promised contract had yet to arrive, I had given little thought to the project, but on the drive from Shepperton to Soho I had produced several promising ideas. I outlined them as vividly as I could.

'Too original,' Hinds commented. Aida agreed. 'Jim, we want that *Drowned World* atmosphere.' She spoke as if this could be sprayed on, presumably in a fetching shade of jungle green.

Hinds then told me what the central idea would be. His secretary had suggested it that morning. This was nothing less than the story of the birth of the Moon – in fact, one of the oldest and corniest ideas in the whole of science fiction, which I would never have dared to lay on his desk. Hines stared hard at me. 'We want you to tell us what happens next.'

I thought desperately, realising that the film industry was not for me. 'A tidal wave?'

'Too many tidal waves. If you've seen one tidal wave you've seen them all.'

A small light came on in the total darkness of my brain. 'But you always see the tidal waves coming in,' I said in a stronger voice. 'We should show the tidal wave going *out*! All those strange creatures and plants…' I ended with a brief course in surrealist biology.

There was a silence as Hinds and Aida stared at each other. I assumed I was about to be shown the door.

'When the wave goes out…' Hinds stood up, clearly rejuvenated, standing behind his huge desk like Captain Ahab sighting the white whale. 'Brilliant. Jim, who's your agent?'

We went out to a glamorous lunch in a restaurant with Roman decor. Hinds and Aida were excited and cheerful, already moving on to the next stage of production, casting the leading characters. I failed to realise it at the time, but I had already reached the high point of my usefulness to them. I should have heard the 'melancholy, long, withdrawing roar' of the ebbing tidal wave, but it was exciting to have an idea taken up so quickly and be plied with enthusiasm, friendship and fine wine. Already they were discussing the complex relationships between the principal characters, difficult to envisage in a film with no dialogue, where emotions were expressed solely in terms of bare-chested men hitting each other with clubs or dragging a handsome blonde into a nearby cave by her hair. In due course I prepared a treatment, some of which survived into the finished film, along with my ebbing wave.

As Hammer films go, it was a success, but I am glad that they misspelled my name in the credits.

In 1986, two years after the publication of *Empire of the Sun*, a very different kind of film company appeared on the scene. Warner Brothers bought the rights to the novel, and asked Steven Spielberg, the world's most successful film-maker, to direct the production. Spielberg at first proposed that he would produce the film, and asked David Lean to direct. But Lean declined, saying that he couldn't handle the boy. Perhaps Jim was too aggressive and too conflicted for Lean, who liked his boy actors to be lisping and slightly effeminate. In any event Spielberg, who had a unique gift for drawing superb performances from child actors, decided to direct it himself.

Most of the film was shot in Shanghai and near Jerez, in Spain, where Lunghua Camp was recreated, but a few scenes were shot in and near London. The Ballard house in Amherst Avenue was divided between three houses in Sunningdale, to the west of London, and Spielberg invited me to play a walk-on part at the fancy-dress party that opens the film. I appeared as John Bull in scarlet coat and top hat. It was on set that I met Spielberg for the first time, and was immediately impressed by his thoughtfulness and his commitment to the novel. Difficult scenes that could easily have been dropped were tackled head-on, like Jim's 'resuscitation' of the young kamikaze pilot who briefly merges into his younger, blazer-wearing self, a powerful image that expresses the essence of the whole novel.

A Spielberg production is a huge event, with hundreds of people involved – technicians, actors, bodyguards, bus drivers and catering staff, publicists and make-up artists. Given the costs involved, the sheer scale of Hollywood films demands the highest degree of professionalism. This is the central paradox of film-making, as far I can see. For hours on the set nothing is happening, but not a second is being wasted. The lighting is in many ways more important than the actors' performances, which can be strengthened by astute cutting and editing. Spielberg, of course, is a master of film narrative, and his films far transcend the performances of individual actors. He told me that he 'saw' the film of *Empire of the Sun* in the scene where the Mustangs are attacking the airfield next to Lunghua Camp, and the fighter aircraft move in slow motion in the eyes of the watching Jim. It's an unsettling moment, one of many in what I think of as Spielberg's best, and most imagined, film.

It was fascinating for me to take part in the Sunningdale scenes, and strange to be involved in a painstakingly accurate recreation of my childhood home. The white telephones and original copies of *Time* magazine, the art deco lamps and rugs, carried me straight back to the Shanghai of the 1930s. The large Sunningdale houses were uncannily similar in their fittings, their door handles and window frames. In fact, the English architects in Shanghai had modelled their Tudor-style houses on the Sunningdale mansions rather than the reverse.

When the fancy-dress party ended, the 'guests' were filmed leaving the house, and I stepped out into the drive to find a line of 1930s American Packards and Buicks, each with a uniformed Chinese chauffeur. The scene was so like the real Shanghai of my childhood that for a moment I fainted.

Other curious reversals occurred during the making of the film. Several of my neighbours in Shepperton worked as extras, drawn by the nearby film studios, and took part in the scenes shot in England. I vividly remember the mother of a girl at the same school as my daughters calling out to me: 'We're going back to Shanghai, Mr Ballard. We're in the film…' I had the uncanny sense that I had chosen to live in Shepperton in 1960 because I knew unconsciously that I would write a novel about Shanghai, and that extras among my neighbours would one day appear in a film based on the novel.

Another eerie moment occurred when I was on the set at Sunningdale, and a 12-year-old boy in fancy dress came up to me and said: 'Hello, Mr Ballard, I'm you.' This was Christian Bale, who played Jim so brilliantly, virtually carrying the whole film on his shoulders. Behind him were two actors in their late thirties, Emily Richard and Rupert Frazer, also in fancy dress, who smiled and said: 'And we're your mother and father.' They were twenty years younger than me at the time, and I had the strange feeling that the intervening years had vanished and I was back in wartime Shanghai.

The Los Angeles premiere of the film in December 1987 was a Hollywood epic in its own right. Claire and I stayed at the Beverly Hilton Hotel, just within sight of the Hollywood sign, where we met Tom Stoppard, the writer of the script, a pleasant but intensely nervous man. Dozens of stars attended the charity screening, some in mink coats, like

Dolly Parton, and others in T-shirts, like Sean Connery. Later the nearby streets were closed to traffic and we walked in procession along red carpets laid in the centre of the road to a vast marquee where a themed banquet was held with Chinese food and Chinese dancers bopping to jive numbers.

In early 1988 my American publisher Farrar Straus arranged a six-city, two-week-long book tour to promote my latest novel. The schedule was exhausting, a non-stop round of interviews, book signings, radio and television appearances. At its best, radio is a thoughtful medium in America, while television is regarded as nothing but a continuous stream of advertising, the programmes included. Publicity and promotion are the air that Americans breathe, and they take it for granted that in every minute of the day someone is trying to sell them something.

Many of my bookshop readings and signings were packed, but others were completely empty, for reasons no one could explain. Americans were unfailingly friendly and helpful, though I noticed an almost universal hostility to Steven Spielberg. One journalist asked me: 'Why did you allow Spielberg to make a film of your novel?' When I replied that he was the greatest film director in America, he promptly corrected me: 'Not the greatest, the most successful.' This was the only time that I've heard success downplayed in America. Usually it marks the end of any argument about the merits or otherwise of a film or book. Perhaps American journalists, who see themselves as the consciences of their nation, resent Spielberg for revealing the sentimental and childlike strains that lie just below the surface of American life. There is certainly a missing dimension that European visitors become aware of within a few days of arrival, a trust in the idea of America that no Frenchman or Briton ever feels about his own country. Or it may be that we in Europe are by nature more depressed.

In London in the spring of 1988 there was a royal command performance of *Empire of the Sun*, attended by Spielberg and Steve Ross, the head of Time Warner and a hugely influential man. I am a lifelong republican and would like to see the monarchy and all hereditary titles abolished, but I was impressed by how hard the Queen worked, making friendly comments to each of us. She was poorly briefed by her English guide, and had to ask Ross what he did, an example of British parochialism (though no fault of the Queen's) at its worst. Cher, among the Hollywood stars in the line-up, suggested to the Queen that she might like to see her own film, *Moonstruck*, then playing on the other side of Leicester Square. Her tone implied that now would be a good time for the Queen to cut and run, if she wanted to see a real movie. It was another extraordinary evening, and one of the strangest sights was the band of the Coldstream Guards marching into the auditorium and the Queen standing to listen to her own anthem. I felt that she was the one person entitled to sit down.

*   *   *

In 1991 I was invited to serve on the jury at MystFest, an Italian film festival of crime and mystery films, which was then held at Viareggio, near the beach where the drowned Shelley was cremated by his friends. The chairman of the jury was Jules Dassin, one of the Hollywood exiles and husband of Melina Mercouri, and the director of *Rififi*, *The Naked City* and other classic noir thrillers. Another of the jurors was Suzanne Cloutier, a former wife of Peter Ustinov who had played Desdemona in Orson Welles's *Othello*. Nick Roeg and Theresa Russell were the guests of honour, and we had a great time in the hotel bar. Claire got on especially well with a young American film-maker of whom none of us had heard; he was screening his first film in a small off-the-beach cinema out of competition. Dassin, a kindly but ailing old man still recovering from open-heart surgery, found him particularly tiring. 'Who is this young man?' he asked me. 'He makes so much noise...' I put out a few feelers and reported back that the young man was called Quentin Tarantino and the film was *Reservoir Dogs*. A year later he was one of the most famous directors in the world.

MystFest was interesting to me because it demonstrated the peculiar psychology of the jury system. The six jurors, with Claire as supernumerary, enjoyed our meals together in Viareggio's best restaurants, including Puccini's favourite. It seemed to me that we were in agreement about everything, sharing the same taste in films, whether European, Japanese or American. I was sure we would come to a speedy conclusion when we sat down to decide on the winner.

Halfway through the festival, when we had seen five films, Jules Dassin called a meeting. 'The films are rubbish,' he told us. 'We'll give the prize to Roeg.' We had not yet seen Roeg's film, *Cold Heaven*, and I pointed out that there were six films waiting to be screened for us. 'They'll be rubbish too,' Dassin said. I suspect that he was under pressure from the festival management to steer the best film award to Roeg. Bob Swaim, the American director of *Half Moon Street* and *La Balance* ('I always sleep with my leading ladies.' This left me agog. 'You've had sex with Sigourney Weaver? Tell me more.' 'No, not Sigourney.') and I insisted that we see all the films, though the other jurors were ready to follow Dassin.

In the event, sadly, Roeg's film was not one of his better efforts, and at our final meeting Dassin gave up his attempt to award the prix d'or to him. But our problems had only just begun. As we discussed the eleven films it soon became clear that we would never agree. Each member of the jury had his or her favourite, which the other jurors dismissed with contempt. We stared at each speaker as if he had announced that he was Napoleon Bonaparte and was about to be taken away by the men in the white coats. Every choice other than my own seemed preposterous. I assume that sitting collectively in judgement runs counter to some deep and innate belief that justice should be dispensed by a single, all-powerful magistrate. How jurors at murder trials ever come to a unanimous verdict is beyond me.

Aware that we were becoming tired and fractious, Dassin wisely called a halt to the discussion. He passed around pieces of paper and asked us each to write down our top three films, in descending order. This we did, and it is remarkable that the eventual winner did not feature in the list of any member of the jury.

Utter deadlock loomed, and tempers rose. No one was prepared to yield an inch. We were saved by one thing alone – our desperate need for lunch. We were tired, angry and starving. At last we seized gratefully on a compromise candidate, a German thriller about a Turkish detective in Berlin. This had been shown without subtitles, and had been barely comprehensible. But it would have to do.

The German woman director was flown in for the prize-giving but the festival organisers were most displeased. Roeg's honour was satisfied, though not in the way we had expected. At the gala evening, in front of massed TV cameras and journalists, we found that our deliberations had been demoted to the status of a 'jury' prize. The festival grand prix, newly created for the occasion, went to Nick Roeg. As the jury retreated from the rear of the stage, well aware of its humiliation, I wished that we had heeded the wise old Jules Dassin and awarded Roeg the prize in the first place.

22

Return to Shanghai (1991)

My novel *The Kindness of Women*, a sequel to *Empire of the Sun*, was published in 1991, and the BBC TV series *Bookmark* decided to make a programme about my life and work. Most of it was filmed in and around Shepperton, but I spent a week in Shanghai with the film crew and its director, James Runcie. He was the son of the then Archbishop of Canterbury, which may have had some bearing on the help that the Chinese gave us. Two English-speaking executives from the Shanghai television service were with us throughout the week. I have no doubt that part of their job was to keep an eye on us, but they went out of their way to lay on an air-conditioned bus and car and smooth our path around any obstacles.

Without their navigation skills we might never have discovered Lunghua Camp, now completely swallowed by the urbanisation of the surrounding countryside. In the 1930s our house in Amherst Avenue had stood on the edge of the western suburbs of Shanghai. Standing on the roof as a boy,

I would look out over the cultivated farmland that began literally on the far side of our garden fence. Now all this had gone, vanishing under the concrete and asphalt of greater Metropolitan Shanghai.

The return to Shanghai, for the only time in forty-five years, was a strange experience for me, which began in the Cathay Pacific lounge at Heathrow. There I saw my first dragon ladies, rich Chinese women with a hard, fear-inducing gaze, similar to those who had known my parents and terrified me as a child. Most of them got off at Hong Kong, but others went on with me to Shanghai. We landed at the International Airport, on one of the huge runways laid across the grass airfield at Hungjao where I had once sat in the cockpit of a derelict Chinese fighter. As the dragon ladies left the first-class compartment their immaculate nostrils twitched disapprovingly at the familiar odour that stained the evening air – night soil, still the chief engine of Chinese agriculture.

We drove into Shanghai down a broad new highway. Lights glimmered through the perspiring trees, and above the microwave air I could see vast skyscrapers built in the 1980s with expat Chinese money. Under Deng's rule, Shanghai was returning rapidly to its great capitalist past. Inside every open doorway a small business was flourishing. A miasma of frying fat floated into the night, radio announcers gabbled, gongs sounded the start or end of a work shift, sparks flew from the lathes of a machine shop, mothers breastfed their babies as they sat patiently by pyramids of melons, traffic horns blared, sweating young men in singlets smoked in doorways ... the ceaseless activity of a planetary hive. There are only two words in the Chinese bible: Make Money.

The Bund was intact, the same vista of banks and trading houses still faced the Whangpoo river, crowded with ships and sampans. The Nanking Road seemed unchanged, Sincere's and the great Sun and Sun Sun department stores crammed with Western goods. The racecourse was now an immense parade ground, the only visible trace of the authoritarian regime. I had hoped that we might stay at the former Cathay Hotel (now the Peace Hotel) on the Bund, a crumbling art deco palace. We later filmed a scene in the karaoke bar, where drunken Japanese tourists bellowed their way through Neil Diamond hits. But the Cathay, where Noël Coward had written *Private Lives*, lacked fax links to the outside world, and we moved to the Shanghai Hilton, a tall tower not far from the former Cathedral Girls' School.

Memories were waiting for me everywhere, like old friends at an arrivals gate, each carrying a piece of cardboard bearing my name. The next morning I looked down at Shanghai from my room on the seventeenth floor of the Hilton. I could see at a glance that there were two Shanghais – the skyscraper city newer than yesterday, and at street level the old Shanghai that I had cycled around as a boy. The Park

Hotel, overlooking the former racecourse and a vast brothel for American servicemen after the war, had been one of the tallest buildings in Shanghai, but was now dwarfed by gigantic TV towers and office buildings that stamped 'money' across the sky. The Hilton stood on the edge of the old French Concession, still today one of the largest collections of domestic art deco architecture in the world. The paintwork was shabby, but there were the porthole windows and marina balconies, fluted pilasters borrowed from some car factory in Detroit in the 1930s. Curiously, the TV towers, broadcasting the new to the people of Shanghai, seemed rather old-fashioned and even traditional, as seen everywhere from Toronto and Tokyo to Seattle. At the same time, the dusty and faded art deco suburbs were bracingly new.

I was due to rendezvous with Runcie and his crew at 9 a.m. in the Hilton lobby, but an hour earlier I slipped out of the hotel and began to walk the streets, heading in the general direction of the Bubbling Well Road. The pavements were already crowded with food vendors, porters steering new photocopiers into office entrances, smartly dressed young secretaries shaking their heads at a plump and sweating 60-year-old European out on some dishevelled errand.

And I was on an errand, though I had yet to grasp the true nature of my assignment. I was looking for my younger self, the boy in a Cathedral School cap and blazer who had played hide-and-seek with his friends half a century earlier. I soon found him, hurrying with me along the Bubbling Well Road, smiling at the puzzled typists and trying to hide the sweat that drenched my shirt. On the last leg of our journey from England, as we took off from Hong Kong, I worried that I had waited too long to return to Shanghai, and that the actual city would never match my memories. But those memories had been remarkably resilient, and I felt surprisingly at home, as if I was about to resume the life cut off when the *Arrawa* set sail from its pier.

But something was missing, and that explained the real nature of my breakfastless errand.

Shanghai had always been a European city, created by British and French entrepreneurs, followed by the Dutch, Swiss and Germans. Now, though, they had gone, and Shanghai was a Chinese city. All the advertising, all the street signs and neon displays, were in Chinese characters. Nowhere, during our week in Shanghai, did I see a single sign in the English language, except for a huge hoarding advertising Kent cigarettes. There were no American cars and buses, no Studebakers and Buicks, no film posters in twenty-foot-high letters announcing *Snow White and the Seven Dwarfs*, *Robin Hood* or *Gone With the Wind*.

Shanghai had forgotten us, as it had forgotten me, and the shabby art deco houses in the French Concession were part of a discarded stage set that was slowly being dismantled. The Chinese are uninterested in the past. The present, and a modest down payment on a first instalment of the future, are all that concern them. Perhaps we in the West are too pre-occupied with the past, too involved with our memories, almost as if we are nervous of the present and want to keep one foot safely rooted in the past. Later, when I left Shanghai and returned to England with Runcie and the film crew, I felt a great sense of release. I had visited those shrines to my younger self, stood in silence for a few moments with my head bowed, and driven straight to the airport.

At 9 on that first morning we gathered in the Hilton lobby and then set off for the Ballard home in the former Amherst Avenue. The house was still standing, though in a state of extreme dilapidation, its gutters propped up by a scaffolding of bamboo poles that was in turn about to collapse. At the time of our visit the house served as the library of a state electronics institute, and metal book-racks filled with inter-national journals and magazines had replaced the furniture on all three floors, a change that might have pleased my father. Nothing, otherwise, had changed, and I noticed that the same lavatory seat was in my bathroom. But the house was a ghost, and had spent almost half a century eroding its memories of an English family that had occupied it but left without a trace.

The next day we set off in our air-conditioned bus for Lunghua, and spent most of the morning trying to track it

The former Ballard house in Amherst Avenue, Shanghai,
in 2005. The fountain, garden sculpture and wall
decoration are recent additions.

down. A vast urbanised plain stretched south from the
Shanghai that I had known, a haze-filled terrain of flats,
factories and police and army barracks, linked together by
motorway overpasses. Now and then we stopped, and
climbed to the roof deck of a workers' apartment block,
where I scanned the countryside for any sight of the water
tower. Eventually, one of our translators hailed an old man
dozing outside a bicycle shop. 'Europeans, imprisoned by the
Japanese...?' He thought about this. 'There was a camp – I
don't remember which war...'

Ten minutes later we arrived at the gates of the former
Lunghua Camp, now the Shanghai High School. Almost

Standing outside the former G Block in 1991.

The Ballard family room in the former G block.

nothing remained of the original camp. The Japanese guard-house, the dozen or more ruined buildings and the wooden huts had all been cleared away. New buildings had been built, and the old ones refurbished.

I wandered around the site for an hour, ignoring my camera but taking a thousand snapshots inside my eye. Everywhere trees had been planted shoulder to shoulder, as a result of some Maoist diktat in the 1960s. The children were away on holiday, and we were able to enter G Block. The Shanghai High School is solely for boarders, and all the rooms were locked except for the former Ballard room, which was now a kind of rubbish store. A clutter of refuse, like discarded memories, lay in sacks between the wooden bed frames, where my mother had read *Pride and Prejudice* for the tenth time, and I had slept and dreamed.

Lunghua Camp was there, but it was not there.

I arrived back at Heathrow feeling mentally bruised but refreshed, as if I had completed the psychological equivalent of an adventure holiday. I had walked up to a mirage, accepted that in its way it was real, and then walked straight through it to the other side. The next ten years were among the most contented of my life.

My daughters Fay and Beatrice had made very happy marriages, and each soon had two children, over whom I doted from the day of their birth. There is no doubt that grandchildren take away the fear of death. I had done my biological duty, and completed the most important task on the genetic job list. My son remains a confirmed bachelor, happy with his computers, his weekend walks and pints of ale.

I was lucky to meet two fellow writers and their lively wives, with whom Claire and I frequently share a meal. Both Iain Sinclair and Will Self are much younger than me, but we fill the gap with shared enthusiasms, and an interest in the world beyond the London literary scene. Sinclair is a poet and mesmerist, tracing out the ley lines of the imagination in his heroic walks around London, making the connections between Templar churches and the archaic ghosts of east London and the Thames Gateway. He is also the Odysseus of the M25, and has walked the 120-mile circuit, threading 19th-century fever hospitals and the graveyards of mysterious parish churches onto his bow. Will Self is another remarkable writer, almost seven feet in height and with a tall man's constant surprise at the mundane world far below him. He is richly generous in thought and speech, forever taking new ideas from the top shelves of his mind and laying. them out in front of you with a flourish. Both Sinclair and Self have a wholly original take on the world, and I have never heard them utter a single cliché or commonplace in all the brilliant books by them that I have read, or in all the meals we have shared together.

I still think about Shanghai, but I know that the city is

Claire Walsh in 1990.

undergoing another of its unending changes. One image that stays in my mind was the glimpse I had of an old man squatting behind a small stool outside the entrance to the Cathay Hotel. He seemed to have nothing for sale, and I couldn't help thinking about another old man under his eiderdown of snow in Amherst Avenue. But this old man seemed confident, and was eating his lunch from a small china bowl, using his chopsticks to fork in a modest portion of rice and a single cabbage leaf.

He was very old, and I wondered if this would be his last meal. Then I looked down at the stool and realised why he was so confident. Lying face up to the passing tourists and office workers, the titles in the Chinese characters of their Hong Kong distributor, were three Arnold Schwarzenegger videos.

23

Homeward Bound (2007)

In June 2006, after a year of pain and discomfort that I put down to arthritis, a specialist confirmed that I was suffering from advanced prostate cancer that had spread to my spine and ribs. Curiously, the only part of my anatomy that did not seem to be affected was my prostate, a common feature of the disease. But an MRI scan, a disagreeable affair that involves lying in a coffin wired for sound, left no doubt. Originating in my prostate, the cancer had invaded my bones.

I moved into the care of Professor Jonathan Waxman, in the Cancer Centre at Hammersmith Hospital in west London. Professor Waxman is one of the leading prostate cancer specialists in this country, and he rescued me at a time when I was exhausted by the intermittent pain and the fears of death that blotted everything else from my mind. It was Jonathan who convinced me that within a few weeks of the initial treatment the pain would leave me and I would begin to feel something closer to my everyday self. This proved true, and for the past year, except for one or two minor relapses, I have felt remarkably well, have been able to work and enjoyed my restaurant visits and the company of friends and family.

Jonathan has always been completely frank, leaving me with no illusions about the eventual end. But he has urged me to lead as normal a life as I can, and he supported me when I said, early in 2007, that I would like to write my auto-biography. It is thanks to Jonathan Waxman that I found the will to write this book.

Jonathan is highly intelligent, thoughtful and always gentle, and has that rare ability to see the ongoing course of medical treatment from the point of view of the patient. I am very grateful that my last days will be spent under the care of this strong-minded, wise and kindly physician.

Shepperton, September 2007